Carey Scott

180 Bible Verses for an

UNSHAKABLE
FAITH

Devotions for Women

BARBOUR
PUBLISHING

Print ISBN 978-1-63609-430-4

Published by Barbour Publishing, Inc., 1810 Barbour Drive, Uhrichsville, Ohio 44683, www.barbourbooks.com

Our mission is to inspire the world with the life-changing message of the Bible.

Member of the
Evangelical Christian
Publishers Association

Printed in China.

Introduction

There is power in God's Word—power to create in every believer an unshakable faith. In its pages, you will be both challenged and encouraged to trust the Lord in every area of your life. Even more, the Bible will give you practical ways to follow God so you can live a righteous life full of joy, peace, strength, and wisdom.

If you're struggling in relationships, let God give you courage through His Word. If you're battling insecurity or hopelessness, dig through scripture to be reminded of your worth. Let His wonderful and inspired words refresh your weary heart when it's overwhelmed. Let it build your confidence and expectation as you wait on the Lord. The Bible is God's love story to the world and is designed to steady your faith for every test and trial that comes your way.

Open its pages to find comfort and guidance. And be ready to meet God in new and meaningful ways.

It's Doubt That Destabilizes

*Jesus replied, "Listen to the truth. If you do not
doubt God's power and speak out of faith's
fullness, you can also speak to a tree and it
will wither away. Even more than that, you
could say to this mountain, 'Be lifted up and
be thrown into the sea' and it will be done."*
MATTHEW 21:21 TPT

Doubt is the great destabilizer of faith. When you question
God's power, you're essentially second-guessing His essence. You're assuming He can't or won't. In your mistrust,
you decide the Lord isn't paying attention to your troubles.
And in the end, you fall back into old habits of control or
worry because you feel unseen by God.

But friend, when you embrace bold faith no matter
what you're facing, you'll become unshakable. Be it valleys
or mountaintops, you'll be secure in the truth of God's
love. And you'll experience His strength running through
your veins.

2

Believing Prayer

"Absolutely everything, ranging from small to large, as you make it a part of your believing prayer, gets included as you lay hold of God."

MATTHEW 21:22 MSG

Praying with belief is vastly different from praying with uncertainty. One is power-packed, while the other is weak-kneed. One allows you to hold on to hope, while the other feeds an unsatisfied and suspicious nature. God is always inviting you to pray with an unwavering belief that He not only hears you but will answer you too. You may not know when or how, but you can be confident the Lord will move for your good and His glory in His perfect timing. When you talk to God, He hears your voice.

So tell God what you need with steadfast faith in His ability and willingness. Wait with patience and expectation. And then pray with gratitude when the answers come.

3

Impossible without Faith

It's impossible to please God apart from faith.
And why? Because anyone who wants
to approach God must believe both that
he exists and that he cares enough to
respond to those who seek him.

HEBREWS 11:6 MSG

Today's verse does not mince words. It's not confusing or unclear. The author tells you straight up that if your faith in God isn't secure, it will be impossible to delight His heart. It isn't meant to be harsh—just honest, so we know without question. As believers, we must understand how important unshakable faith is to the Lord. It's the foundation that holds us tight when life feels overwhelming. Without it, we'll find ourselves adrift.

Today, make sure you not only believe He is real but also trust He will respond to those who love Him. Choose to believe God is faithful in all things. And let those truths make your faith unshakable!

4

Faith from Hearing

*So faith proceeds from hearing, as we listen
to the message about God's Anointed.*
ROMANS 10:17 VOICE

Scripture says that God's Word is so powerful that when we hear His message, it has the ability to birth new faith in an unbeliever. It can open eyes and soften hearts to the Good News. Even more, it often strengthens what little faith we may already have, giving us an immovable trust in God's sovereignty.

Consider then how important it is that we are willing to share our testimony when the opportunity arises. It may be what leads someone to a believing faith in the Lord or what empowers them to return to God as they navigate their difficult circumstances. Every day, ask for courage to tell others how He has moved in your life. Let them know God will respond to their needs, whether big or small. Friend, be committed to encouraging another to believe in God's promises.

5

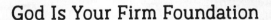

God Is Your Firm Foundation

*The fundamental fact of existence is that this
trust in God, this faith, is the firm foundation
under everything that makes life worth living.
It's our handle on what we can't see.*

HEBREWS 11:1 MSG

When life feels chaotic and out of control, we all look for
something to hold on to. Some may cling to certain people
in their life, mistaking them as saviors. Others may reach
for an addiction or something that helps numb their fear
and worry. Still others may rely on their own strength and
wisdom, making decisions that feel right in the moment.
But when we place our faith in God, we can be assured
that the foundation is firm and unmovable.

Where do you go when storms hit your life? Whom
do you trust the most? What is the Holy Spirit speaking
to you about that right now?

6

Believe and Speak It Out

So if you believe deep in your heart that God raised Jesus from the pit of death and if you voice your allegiance by confessing the truth that "Jesus is Lord," then you will be saved!
ROMANS 10:9 VOICE

If you want to anchor your faith to truth, knowing your salvation is secured with God in heaven, then let today's passage of scripture lead you into a saving prayer. Tell the Lord you believe He raised Jesus from the dead. Tell Him you recognize your sin and your need for a Savior. And thank Him that Jesus' death brings redemptive power into your life.

Then, friend, share this good news with the world. Embrace every opportunity to boast about His goodness. Let your voice proclaim the magnificence of God's transformative power. And be ready to explain the joy and peace your life reflects. Tell others why your faith in God is unshakable!

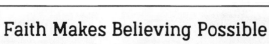

1

Faith Makes Believing Possible

Faith empowers us to see that the universe was created and beautifully coordinated by the power of God's words! He spoke and the invisible realm gave birth to all that is seen.

HEBREWS 11:3 TPT

There are some things in the Bible that feel fantastical. Some stories seem outlandish and hard to imagine. We wonder how Noah built the ark and how the animals showed up in twos. We are awestruck by imagining the Red Sea parting and the Israelites crossing on dry land. Knowing Daniel spent the night in the lions' den without harm is unbelievable. And realizing God literally spoke the earth and the universe into existence is mind-blowing.

But scripture says it's your faith that allows you to believe all that God has done, all that He has created, and the powerful stories shared in His Word. Your faith is what makes your ability to believe in His will and ways. . .unwavering.

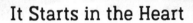

8

It Starts in the Heart

*Belief begins in the heart and leads to a life
that's right with God; confession departs
from our lips and brings eternal salvation.*

ROMANS 10:10 VOICE

Believing with your heart is what makes the difference. Sometimes, we put all the value on logic. We think knowing in our minds is the most important thing. But God wants your heart to be for Him. When you confess your sins and your need for a Savior—when you accept Jesus' redemptive act on the cross—it gives you unshakable faith. Your salvation can't be lost.

So, friend, make sure you connect to God from the heart and not just from your head. Feel the weight of His compassion on your life. Watch for the movement of His hand in your circumstances. Meditate on His love and goodness. And then let those powerful feelings flood your heart so you can fully embrace the gift of Jesus.

9

The World or the Father

Don't love the world's ways. Don't love the world's goods. Love of the world squeezes out love for the Father. Practically everything that goes on in the world—wanting your own way, wanting everything for yourself, wanting to appear important—has nothing to do with the Father. It just isolates you from him.

1 JOHN 2:15-16 MSG

Every day you have a choice to make. You can either give in to the pull of the world and embrace its offerings, or you can turn your face toward God and live by faith. While this decision seems easy on paper, it's often a difficult decision to make in real time.

The truth is you can't serve the world and the Father at the same time. While the things of this earth look promising, God is the only One who can make good on every promise. . .every time. And it's that perfect track record that makes your faith unshakable.

10

Big Prayers

"Listen to the truth I speak to you: Whoever says to this mountain with great faith and does not doubt, 'Mountain, be lifted up and thrown into the midst of the sea,' and believes that what he says will happen, it will be done."

MARK 11:23 TPT

There are certain times when our prayer requests require massive answers. Maybe it's healing from a terminal illness or a financial blessing so filing for bankruptcy isn't the next step. Maybe it's a job after months of unemployment or the restoration of a relationship battered by betrayal.

Regardless, you have the freedom to ask for big things from God! Scripture says you can even tell a mountain to be thrown into the sea, and if you have unshakable faith, it will happen. Do not be afraid to ask for what you need. Be confident. Be bold. And be steadfast as you approach the throne.

11

Obeying without the Details

By faith Noah respected God's warning regarding the flood—the likes of which no one had ever seen—and built an ark that saved his family. In this he condemned the world and inherited the righteousness that comes by faith.
HEBREWS 11:7 VOICE

Don't miss the powerful nugget in today's scripture. Noah acted on God's request of him without understanding all the particulars surrounding it. He didn't require a detailed explanation. He didn't need to know how all the pieces would come together. Noah recognized God's sovereignty and his need for obedience, so he simply said yes.

You can be faithful by following the same formula. Choose to obey because you choose to trust God's will and ways. Most of the time, we are on a *need-to-know* basis. And we can walk that out with confidence because we trust the One leading the way.

12

Boldly Asking

"This is the reason I urge you to boldly believe for whatever you ask for in prayer—be convinced that you have received it and it will be yours."

MARK 11:24 TPT

Don't be wimpy as you pray. Don't be shy in asking for God's help. And don't ask while convinced He won't answer. As a believer, pray with conviction. You can boldly go to God in prayer and share your hopes and desires. Even more, when you ask with the right motives for the Lord to intervene in your circumstances, He will bless your requests with a loving response.

Do you need hope? Are you desperate for peace? Do you need divine wisdom and discernment? Are you lacking joy? Do you need self-control? Do you need a shift in perspective or a renewal of your mind? Ask God with humility, and then choose to be convinced He's already given it to you.

13

When He Calls You

*By faith Abraham heard God's call to travel
to a place he would one day receive as an
inheritance; and he obeyed, not knowing
where God's call would take him.*
HEBREWS 11:8 VOICE

Are you listening for God's voice in your life? Chances are it won't be audible but rather a discernment in your spirit. You will feel a leading. A prompting. You'll experience a tug of the heart one way or another. And when you do—just like Abraham—respond with obedience.

God knows the specifics of the path He's calling you to walk. His plans include sustaining you each step of the way. In His wisdom, God is preparing the details of the destination. And as you press into the process with unshakable faith, you'll find a deeper connection with the Lord. Friend, you can trust the Father with it all.

14

Nothing Will Be Too Much

Jesus was matter-of-fact: "Embrace this God-life. Really embrace it, and nothing will be too much for you."

MARK 11:22 MSG

What would it look like for you to fully embrace your faith? What would have to change for you to surrender to God, allowing Him to determine your next steps? Jesus is making a beautiful promise in today's scripture. He is encouraging believers to grab hold of a faith-filled life because divine strength and wisdom come with it. We do that by spending time in the Word, praying with fervor, and finding like-minded community to do life with.

The truth is we're not guaranteed an easy life just because we follow Jesus. The valleys and pits won't be unavoidable. But when we feel overwhelmed, scared, or hopeless, our faith will carry us through. We will find the strength and the perseverance to stand strong. We will be immovable.

15

Tapped into His Faithfulness

Sarah's faith embraced God's miracle power to conceive even though she was barren and was past the age of childbearing, for the authority of her faith rested in the One who made the promise, and she tapped into his faithfulness.

HEBREWS 11:11 TPT

Can you imagine the kind of faith it took to believe through impossibility? Not only had Sarah been unable to have children, but she was also years past childbearing age. Yet—and remarkably—she tapped into the faithfulness of God and believed through Him. In the natural, it looked impossible, but her steadfast faith created a different scenario.

You can harness that same kind of faith. Don't be convinced of defeat. Instead, tap into God's faithfulness because He is your authority. He has the last word. And when you put your trust in what He says, even when circumstances seem hopeless, your faith will be rock solid.

16

Saved by Faith Alone

For by grace you have been saved by faith. Nothing you did could ever earn this salvation, for it was the love gift from God that brought us to Christ! So no one will ever be able to boast, for salvation is never a reward for good works or human striving.

EPHESIANS 2:8-9 TPT

It's a blessing that we are saved by faith through God's grace. He knew we would be unable to fulfill the requirements for salvation, so He graciously removed the burden from us. Instead, it was Jesus who made a way through His death and resurrection.

Let this stabilize your heart, recognizing there's nothing you can do aside from accepting Jesus as your Savior. It doesn't matter how much money you give, how often you volunteer, or if you're full of compassion. Good works don't open the door to eternity for anyone. Anchor your faith in this truth so it's unshakable.

17

Promises Will Be Fulfilled

These heroes all died still clinging to
their faith, not even receiving all that
had been promised them. But they saw
beyond the horizon the fulfillment of their
promises and gladly embraced it from
afar. They all lived their lives on earth as
those who belonged to another realm.
HEBREWS 11:13 TPT

Today's scripture asks us to consider that some of God's promises may not come to fruition in our lifetime. It may be others who see the beauty of the promise fulfilled that we prayed for.

What are you praying for right now? The return of a wayward child? The salvation of a good friend? A revival in the church or restoration of the nation? Be persistent in your prayers, asking for your heart's desire and knowing His faithfulness. Just because your eyes may not witness His answers doesn't mean they won't come to pass. And, friend, your dedication in asking never goes unnoticed.

18

While You Were Still Wretched

*But God still loved us with such great love.
He is so rich in compassion and mercy. Even
when we were dead and doomed in our many
sins, he united us into the very life of Christ
and saved us by his wonderful grace!*

EPHESIANS 2:4–5 TPT

You can have unshakable faith in God because of His unwavering dedication. He was so committed to bridging the gap left by sin that His Son made a way for us to be with Him forever. In His compassion and mercy, the Father sent Jesus to the cross so we could be made clean.

There's no one who would (or could) love so lavishly. No one is more devoted to those who love Him. And it's because God is rich in mercy that He promised to save by grace while we were wretched. When you're sold out for Him, it's a time-tested decision based on a time-trusted God.

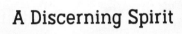

19

A Discerning Spirit

Faith prompted the parents of Moses at his
birth to hide him for three months, because
they realized their child was exceptional and
they refused to be afraid of the king's edict.
HEBREWS 11:23 TPT

Sometimes what God asks of us is different from what the law of the land may be. You can see this in the story of Moses. The king's law said all newborn boys would be killed, but God had other plans. So rather than follow the edict, his parents hid him.

It takes divine wisdom and discernment when it comes to going against those in authority. We must guard against using it to justify bad or disrespectful behavior. And we have to listen to the Holy Spirit showing us God's will in certain situations. Your loyalty is to the Lord above all else, so ask for a discerning spirit to know the right thing to do.

20

A Fully Loved Creation

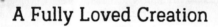

Instead, we are God's accomplishment,
created in Christ Jesus to do good things.
God planned for these good things to
be the way that we live our lives.

EPHESIANS 2:10 CEB

Because we are God's thoughtful and fully loved creation, we can safely anchor our faith in the One who designed us. Because He planned good things for our life before we even took our first breath on earth, we can trust His perfect plan each day. Our steadfast faith comes directly from a relationship with our steadfast Father.

Today, ask God to give you a fresh revelation of who He is. Let Him affirm your immeasurable value through His eyes. It's when we understand who the Father is in relation to who we are that we develop a powerful believing faith. It's not just a prayer of salvation; it's a lifelong commitment to live dedicated to the Lord.

21

Struggling to Trust

Faith opened the way for the Hebrews to cross the Red Sea as if on dry land, but when the Egyptians tried to cross they were swallowed up and drowned!
HEBREWS 11:29 TPT

The story of the Israelites' exodus out of slavery in Egypt is a powerful story of God's sovereignty. One of the most remarkable and beautiful ways God showed His love is captured in the Red Sea moment. With a giant body of water in front of them and an angry Egyptian army chasing them from behind, they had no option but to trust God's deliverance. And the Lord made a way, just like He always does.

While this should have given the Israelites unshakable faith, it did not. They struggled to trust His provision and goodness throughout their years in the wilderness. Let's choose to be women secure in the promises of God. Let's choose to believe He will do what He promises every time.

22

Living Here and Longing for There

That's why we're always full of courage.
Even while we're at home in the body, we're
homesick to be with the Master—for we live
by faith, not by what we see with our eyes.
2 Corinthians 5:6-7 tpt

Even with the world feeling crazy right now, we're able to live with confidence because we know our home is in heaven. We don't have to give in to fear of the future. Worry and anxiety don't need to be part of our day. And there's no reason for us to embrace instability and insecurity, because our faith provides a firm foundation. Through it, our heart is strengthened, and we're made brave as we navigate life here while longing for eternity there.

Ask the Lord for divine perspective to see the bigger picture. It's normal to long for heaven as we find peace here. The two can coexist and keep our faith steady.

23

Fearlessly Faithful

*By faith, the Israelites marched around the walls
of Jericho for seven days, and the walls fell flat.*
HEBREWS 11:30 MSG

We've been talking about the beauty of having unshakable faith for ourselves, but consider that our faith may cause the shaking for others too. Think about it. Out of obedience, the Israelites followed the craziest battle plan ever designed. They blew trumpets and walked in circles around the city. The people of Jericho must have laughed and mocked. But God's people walked it out to a *T*, and as promised, the walls of Jericho began to shake and then fell to the ground.

That's what unwavering belief can do. When we're all in for following God, our faith is empowered to move mountains and shake walls and pave the way for breathtaking miracles. Never underestimate the sovereignty of God and the power He gives to those who choose to be fearlessly faithful.

24

Tightly Held

*For it is Christ's love that fuels our passion and
holds us tightly, because we are convinced
that he has given his life for all of us.*

2 CORINTHIANS 5:14 TPT

When we truly believe in the saving work of Jesus and what it affords to believers, it changes us. A heart of gratitude will empower us to fill our lives with passion and purpose, grabbing hold of the calling God put on our lives before the beginning of time. And we will desire the pursuit of righteous living and growing our relationship with the Father.

But notice the beautiful promise mentioned in today's verse. The Lord's love will wrap around you tightly as you embrace Jesus and the gift of salvation. Your staunch belief in the finished work of Jesus will bless you with a deeper awareness of His presence, and your unshakable faith will delight God's heart.

25

The Telltale of Good Works

*My dear brothers and sisters, what good
is it if someone claims to have faith but
demonstrates no good works to prove it?
How could this kind of faith save anyone?*

JAMES 2:14 TPT

When you become a believer, there's a beautiful transformation that happens. Your old ways are replaced with the pursuit of righteous living. You think differently. You act differently. The Holy Spirit inside helps you discern right from wrong. And you will want your new way of living to be evidence of your faith.

Take some time to digest today's scripture. Be introspective, looking at your life for the *good works* that demonstrate your belief. Ask God to meet you in that moment to confirm or convict. There's nothing we can do to work our way into heaven, but the good work we do will prove that's where we will spend eternity.

26

When We Face Tests

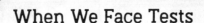

My brothers and sisters, think of the various
tests you encounter as occasions for joy.
After all, you know that the testing of your
faith produces endurance. Let this endurance
complete its work so that you may be fully
mature, complete, and lacking in nothing.
JAMES 1:2-4 CEB

The only way we can have unshakable faith is through God's help. On our own, we can be brave for a bit. We can be courageous for a while. But our confidence will eventually wane. And when that happens, we'll be left struggling with fear and worry. Trusting God through the tests will do some deep work in the believer. We'll discover these difficult moments don't have to pull us under. Scripture even says we can have joy through it.

Testing is necessary because it creates endurance that matures our faith. And it's that established faith that proves unshakable when our world gets rocked.

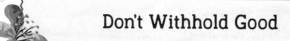

27

Don't Withhold Good

*The LORD will be your confidence; he will
guard your feet from being snared. Don't
withhold good from someone who deserves
it, when it is in your power to do so.*

PROVERBS 3:26–27 CEB

In a world that can sometimes feel hopeless and harsh, do good when the opportunity presents itself. It doesn't have to be perfect or lavish. You don't have to go overboard to prove a point or impress others. But out of gratitude for God's protection in your life, be His hands and feet in the lives of others.

Take a meal to a family battling health issues. Mow the lawn or shovel the driveway of an aging neighbor. Financially support a cause that furthers the Gospel. Compliment appropriately and whenever possible. And when your faith is being nudged to be bold, don't ignore it. Instead, act on His prompting every time you feel it.

28

Asking without Doubt or Hesitation

Whoever asks shouldn't hesitate. They should ask in faith, without doubting. Whoever doubts is like the surf of the sea, tossed and turned by the wind.

JAMES 1:6 CEB

When you have a need, scripture says to not hesitate asking God for help. When someone comes to you desperate for the Lord to move in their circumstances, pray right then and there. Prayer is a gift from God, so always bow your head with confidence, knowing He is listening.

As a believer, you can talk to God directly, not having to pray through someone else or follow any formula. He invites you to share with Him anytime and anywhere. And even more, scripture tells us to petition God with a firm belief and without hesitancy. It's not with a cocky attitude or feeling like God works for us. Instead, it's demonstrating an unshakable faith, which is sure to settle our anxious heart and bring peace.

29

Enabled by the Spirit

*Everything we could ever need for life and
godliness has already been deposited in us
by his divine power. For all this was lavished
upon us through the rich experience of
knowing him who has called us by name
and invited us to come to him through a
glorious manifestation of his goodness.*

2 PETER 1:3 TPT

God places in us the ability to live righteously. What a
blessing, since we recognize our sinful nature and are
acutely aware of the limitations our humanity battles
every day.

We aren't born with this ability. When we accept Jesus
as our Savior and place our faith in the Father, the Holy
Spirit is deposited inside us. In that very moment, we're
given the One who will guide us through the ups and downs
of life and enable godliness. And as the Spirit matures our
faith and we deepen our relationship with God, our faith
will become steadfast.

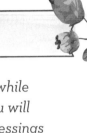

30

Strong Faith

*If your faith remains strong, even while
surrounded by life's difficulties, you will
continue to experience the untold blessings
of God! True happiness comes as you pass
the test with faith, and receive the victorious
crown of life promised to every lover of God!*

JAMES 1:12 TPT

It's easy to say you believe in God when you're happy and life is smooth. But when difficulties arise and you cling to the Lord, you'll be blessed in the mess. Acting faith-filled when life is smooth takes no effort at all. But you will know the authenticity of your belief when the storms come rolling in.

With anchored faith that God is at work, unexplainable peace will blanket you even as your world turns upside down. Rather than expect an earthly savior, you'll cling to *the* Savior. And no matter how bad the shaking, true happiness will result from your strong faith.

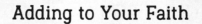

31

Adding to Your Faith

*This is why you must make every effort to
add moral excellence to your faith; and to
moral excellence, knowledge; and to knowledge,
self-control; and to self-control, endurance; and to
endurance, godliness; and to godliness, affection
for others; and to affection for others, love.*

2 Peter 1:5–7 CEB

When we add these to our faith, we'll escape the pull of the world. We won't fall prey to its immorality or feed the craving for sin. Making time with God a priority will deepen your desire to live in a right relationship with Him and not the world.

There's an enemy who wants to derail your faith and make you inactive and unfruitful. And he does this by coming between you and the Father. Ask God to make your faith unflinching so you can enjoy a life full of God's blessing, knowing your words and actions delight the Lord's heart as they point others to Him.

32

God Doesn't Tempt You

When you are tempted don't ever say, "God is tempting me," for God is incapable of being tempted by evil and he is never the source of temptation. Instead it is each person's own desires and thoughts that drag them into evil and lure them away into darkness.

JAMES 1:13-14 TPT

Temptation will never come from the Lord. It's designed to make you sin, keeping you from righteous living. We're tempted because our fleshly desires are preyed upon by the enemy, whose plan is to exploit every opportunity to discourage and destroy.

But God—in an effort to grow your faith—uses tests and trials. These are God-ordained to help you learn who He is in your life and who you are because of Him. They are always for your good and God's glory. In the end, they help create a stable faith that's immovable when you are tested.

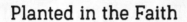

33

Planted in the Faith

*Now He has reconciled you in His body—
in His flesh through His death—so that He
can present you to God holy, blameless,
and totally free of imperfection as long
as you stay planted in the faith.*

Colossians 1:22–23 voice

The bushes in your yard or trees in the forest will wither and die if they're uprooted from the ground. They need the soil to provide nutrients and water for growth and survival. And their roots in the soil hold them secure, able to weather wind and storms.

When today's scripture mentions staying planted in the faith, what does it mean to you? Maybe it means regular time in the Word, looking for wisdom and discernment in its pages. Maybe you weave prayer throughout the day as you seek strength and hope. Discover what keeps you planted in the faith, and let it secure you firmly in God.

34

The Struggle to Trust

*Every gift God freely gives us is good and
perfect, streaming down from the Father
of lights, who shines from the heavens
with no hidden shadow or darkness
and is never subject to change.*

JAMES 1:17 TPT

Your faith in God can be unshakable because there's a guarantee He is immovable. Maybe you struggle with trust because people have been unreliable in the past. Maybe you've encountered deceit and dishonesty from those you depended on. So the idea of trusting that God is good and faithful feels destabilizing.

But the undeniable Word of God clearly says He has "no hidden shadow or darkness." He has no ulterior motive, nor is He trying to deceive you in any way. And even more, God can't change, which means He brings the gift of stability to the relationship. You can trust the Lord to be reliable above everyone else.

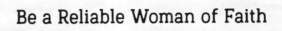

35

Be a Reliable Woman of Faith

*If you're faithful in small-scale matters, you'll
be faithful with far bigger responsibilities.
If you're crooked in small responsibilities,
you'll be no different in bigger things.*

LUKE 16:10 VOICE

God is looking for trustworthy servants to further His
message and kingdom here on earth. His plan to spread
the Gospel has always been based on the willingness of
believers to spread the Good News throughout the world.
And every time you prove yourself dependable with the
small tasks set before you, God takes note.

Ask Him to help make you a reliable woman of faith.
Ask God to place in you a steadfast desire to follow His
leading and prompting. Show consistency with what you
say and how you live, because your choices preach too.
And be ready for a greater responsibility, committed to
showing your Father in heaven trustworthiness in the
calling placed on your life.

36

Absorbing God's Word

This is why we abandon everything morally
impure and all forms of wicked conduct.
Instead, with a sensitive spirit we absorb
God's Word, which has been implanted
within our nature, for the Word of Life
has power to continually deliver us.

JAMES 1:21 TPT

How do you *absorb* God's Word? Maybe it's sitting in a passage of scripture, meditating on its meaning. Maybe it's digging into commentaries or looking up verses in the original language. Maybe it's discussing with friends, looking for hidden meaning and deeper insight. Or maybe it's asking God for fresh revelation to understand what He wants you to glean.

Regardless, this exercise will create in you an unshakable faith as you learn the power of God's Word in your life. You'll find a boldness to trust His will and ways. And you'll discover its "power to continually deliver" you, no matter what comes your way.

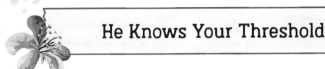

37

He Knows Your Threshold

*No test or temptation that comes your way
is beyond the course of what others have
had to face. All you need to remember is that
God will never let you down; he'll never let
you be pushed past your limit; he'll always
be there to help you come through it.*

1 CORINTHIANS 10:13 MSG

What a beautiful revelation to realize God will never push you past your limit. He won't ever let you down. And even more, God promises to be with you always, helping you through every difficulty you face. Friend, He is trustworthy!

You see, because God created you with great thought and intention, He knows your threshold. He is well aware of the state of your heart and recognizes your boundaries. And when you cling to Him through the hard moments, God won't let you fall. Let Him build in you a steadfast faith that trusts without fail. Ask for it.

38

Be a Doer

*Don't just listen to the Word of Truth and
not respond to it, for that is the essence of
self-deception. So always let his Word become
like poetry written and fulfilled by your life!*

JAMES 1:22 TPT

So often, we listen to a great sermon or read scripture that moves our heart, and rather than put it into action, we let it slip away. We feel its weight but fail to grab hold of it with fervor. It's not that we don't hear God speaking; we just don't document it in meaningful ways.

God wants His Word to be like poetry demonstrated throughout our life. Once we allow it to be written on our heart, we can then let it flow through the words we say and the things we do. Every day, our life can reveal unshakable faith in the Lord. Be a doer of the Word, not just a listener.

39

His Loyal and Merciful Love

GOD's loyal love couldn't have run out, his merciful love couldn't have dried up. They're created new every morning. How great your faithfulness! I'm sticking with GOD (I say it over and over). He's all I've got left.
LAMENTATIONS 3:22–24 MSG

When you're at the end of your rope and feel as though you have nothing left, God is still there. You can't run Him off or exasperate Him. Actually, there's nothing you can do to make the Lord love you any more or any less than He does in this moment. And scripture says God renews His love for you every morning.

So, you can completely trust God with your heart. You can tell Him everything—the good, the bad, and the ugly—and know His loyal and merciful love hasn't changed. Ask God to help you believe that He is and will always be a constant in your life, no matter what.

40

Designed to Make a Difference

*True spirituality that is pure in the eyes of our
Father God is to make a difference in the lives of
the orphans, and widows in their troubles, and
to refuse to be corrupted by the world's values.*

JAMES 1:27 TPT

Your life is designed to make a difference. When God created you, He determined a calling on your life, something He planned in advance for you to walk out on this earth. Make no mistake, you're here for a reason. And as you embrace this powerful truth, it'll help you become committed to living a faithful life.

So, friend, be a fierce lover of people. Look for opportunities to be His hands and feet. Commit to helping others whenever possible. Be ready to insert yourself into situations when God requires your time, talent, or treasure. Ask the Lord for steadfast faith so you can obey without question and act without hesitation.

41

Put God in the Driver's Seat

*Trust GOD from the bottom of your heart;
don't try to figure out everything on your
own. Listen for GOD's voice in everything you
do, everywhere you go; he's the one who will
keep you on track. Don't assume that you
know it all. Run to GOD! Run from evil!*

PROVERBS 3:5–7 MSG

It takes dedicated faith to trust God when things are going okay. But when life feels out of control, it takes unshakable faith to put God in the driver's seat. Because it's our natural response, we try to fix things ourselves. We ruminate over conversations and obsess over details. But scripture tells us to surrender our control habit and instead rely on God.

It may take every bit of strength, but have steadfast faith as you choose to believe God will keep you on track. And pray with confidence, knowing He will guide your steps.

42

The First and the Best

*Honor GOD with everything you own; give
him the first and the best. Your barns will
burst, your wine vats will brim over.*

PROVERBS 3:9–10 MSG

Because God has been so gracious to us, we should be gracious to Him. Scripture says that every good thing comes from God, so the idea of honoring Him with *the first and the best* should be consistent with a heart of gratitude. And because He rewards obedience, it should be no surprise God blesses our act of thankfulness with abundance.

This kind of mindset reveals unwavering faith in God. To think this way and respond without hesitation proves a heart surrendered to the Lord. What a privilege to serve God with our first and best. He is so kind and generous to those who love Him. Let God be what delights your heart, and know you are what delights His too!

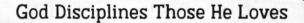

43

God Disciplines Those He Loves

But don't, dear friend, resent GOD's discipline;
don't sulk under his loving correction.
It's the child he loves that GOD corrects;
a father's delight is behind all this.

PROVERBS 3:11–12 MSG

Just like any good parent would do, God disciplines those He loves. He offers loving correction because He values you, and He desires the very best for His beloved. Friend, your heavenly Father wants to steer you clear of needless pain and heartache. God wants to keep you focused on the beautiful path He planned for long ago. And the Lord loves you too much to leave you to your own devices.

So when God intervenes, don't be angry. When He closes a door without warning, don't build a heart of resentment. Instead, anchor your faith in praises! Remember, you are deeply loved by the One who created you, and He is not willing to stand by and watch you flail and falter.

44

The Faithfulness of God

*Count on this: God is faithful and in
His faithfulness called you out into
an intimate relationship with His Son,
our Lord Jesus the Anointed.*
1 CORINTHIANS 1:9 VOICE

There may not be much you can bank on today, but you can forever bank on God's faithfulness. The Lord has your back forever and always. He has amazing plans for your one and only life—plans He determined before you took your first breath on planet Earth. And once you accept salvation through His Son, Jesus Christ, and your name is written in the Lamb's Book of Life, you can rest knowing nothing can snatch you from His hands.

God's desire is for you to pursue Him every day. Through prayer and time in the Word, the Lord wants an intimate relationship with His beloved. And it will create an unshakable faith that will keep you secure through the ups and downs of life.

45

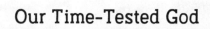

Our Time-Tested God

So let's do it—full of belief, confident that
we're presentable inside and out. Let's
keep a firm grip on the promises that keep
us going. He always keeps his word.

HEBREWS 10:22-23 MSG

You learn to trust someone because of their caring and constant behavior over time. You make note of how their words and actions line up on the regular. And once trust has been established, even if they make a bad judgment call or fall short in some way, you're able to lean on your firm belief their heart for you is always good.

While it may take time to establish trust in the natural, that testing period doesn't apply to God. The Word tells us He is the same yesterday, today, and tomorrow. And since God and His Word are unchanging, the promises in the Bible are for us too. Your faith can be unshakable because the Lord is time-tested and proved to be faithful!

46

God's Economy

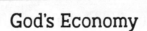

He chose the lowly, the laughable in the world's eyes—nobodies—so that he would shame the somebodies. For he chose what is regarded as insignificant in order to supersede what is regarded as prominent, so that there would be no place for prideful boasting in God's presence.

1 Corinthians 1:28–29 tpt

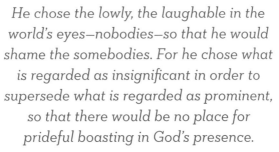

In God's economy, things are always different from what the world says is normal. Here, it's all about fitting in, keeping up with the Joneses, making a splash, collecting toys, and staying up on the latest trends. The world tells you these things matter, leaving us to strive toward them so we're accepted.

But God doesn't care about those things. He sees them as distractions from what's really important. Instead, God looks at the heart. And when we're trying to keep up with the world, our faith suffers. Pursue God over all else. Let Him anchor you in His promises.

47

Being an Encouragement to Others

Let's see how inventive we can be in encouraging
love and helping out, not avoiding worshiping
together as some do but spurring each other on,
especially as we see the big Day approaching.
HEBREWS 10:24–25 MSG

Consider that God may be using you to help others develop unshakable faith. He wants us to look for new and fresh ways to make a difference. Our purposes and passion for the kingdom may be unique and different, but encouraging others is universal. Lending a hand to those in need is part of the collective spirit. Even more, spending time together in community is a common calling that knits us together as believers.

Ask God to open your eyes and sharpen your hearing. Look and listen for ways to spur others on because Jesus is coming back! And in this unsettling world, we need reminders that God is real and our faith in Him can be steadfast.

48

Faith over Fear

He also says, "My righteous ones will live from my faith. But if fear holds them back, my soul is not content with them!" But we are certainly not those who are held back by fear and perish; we are among those who have faith and experience true life!

HEBREWS 10:38–39 TPT

Have you faced fear recently? Maybe the dreaded phone call came, or you discovered a betrayal. Maybe you were overwhelmed by an old memory triggered by a new situation. Maybe the bills are overwhelming. Friend, did you invite God into those moments?

The Lord wants us to live by faith—the kind of faith that's immovable by the scary moments in life. And this is only possible through time spent in the Word and in prayer with our magnificent Father. Ask Him to build in you a firm foundation of faith that will help you experience peace when fear creeps in.

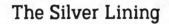

49

The Silver Lining

*I want you to know, dear ones, what has
happened to me has not hindered, but helped
my ministry of preaching the gospel, causing
it to expand and spread to many people.*

PHILIPPIANS 1:12 TPT

Talk about an eternal perspective! This was part of Paul's letter to the Philippians, written from a dark and dank jail cell. He wasn't comfy at home watching Netflix. He didn't just finish a yummy meal at his favorite restaurant. Instead, Paul was in prison, locked up for spreading the Gospel.

Because he fearlessly trusted God, Paul was able to see the big picture. He realized his imprisonment had a silver lining. He recognized the message of hope could not be stopped. Let this challenge us to see our difficulties from an eternal perspective. When we fully believe God is trustworthy, our circumstances won't shake us. Like Paul, we'll see the silver lining too.

50

Your Life Preaches

And what I'm going through has actually caused many believers to become even more courageous in the Lord and to be bold and passionate to preach the Word of God, all because of my chains.

PHILIPPIANS 1:14 TPT

Can you remember somebody whose faith moved you? No matter what, they believed God for a miracle. They spent hours on their knees in prayer. They dug through the Word looking for gold nuggets to cling to. And remember how their faith strengthened you to trust God in your own difficulties?

Never forget your life preaches. People watch how you navigate mountaintops and valleys. And your unshakable faith might be just what others need to see so they can have much-needed hope God will show up for them too. Be ready and willing to share His goodness. We all need a reminder God loves us and is for us.

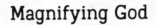

Magnifying God

No matter what, I will continue to hope and passionately cling to Christ, so that he will be openly revealed through me before everyone's eyes. So I will not be ashamed! In my life or in my death, Christ will be magnified in me.

PHILIPPIANS 1:20 TPT

Consider that we are here to magnify Christ to the world. We should live in such a way that others are compelled by our life. They should notice the hope we have when things are hard. We should be transparent about the times God has saved us. When life is chaotic, our peace should be visible, and our compassion for the downtrodden and heartbroken should be evident.

People need to know there's a better way, and Christ is the answer. Let them see your commitment to an unwavering faith. Be intentional to demonstrate a loving relationship with God, being honest about the power He brings into your life.

52

It's a Privilege

Then you will never be shaken or intimidated by the opposition that rises up against us. Your courage will prove to be a sure sign from God of their coming destruction. For God has graciously given you the privilege not only to believe in Christ, but also to suffer for him.

PHILIPPIANS 1:28–29 TPT

This is a tough verse to read, especially when you're in a season of suffering. Imagine someone telling you what a privilege it is to agonize and ache like Jesus did. In your grief, that's the last way you would be feeling, right? But when you have unshakable faith, that's exactly the perspective you can have.

You won't curl into a ball or hide under the covers. You won't wave the white flag and give up. Instead, you'll have courage, knowing God is working on your behalf. And your confidence will be firm, realizing He's with you.

53

When Loving Is Hard

*Love is patient; love is kind. Love isn't envious,
doesn't boast, brag, or strut about. There's
no arrogance in love; it's never rude, crude,
or indecent—it's not self-absorbed. Love isn't
easily upset. Love doesn't tally wrongs or
celebrate injustice; but truth—yes, truth—is
love's delight! Love puts up with anything
and everything that comes along; it trusts,
hopes, and endures no matter what.*

1 CORINTHIANS 13:4–7 VOICE

This kind of love is difficult at best to walk out. Even with those we adore, we'll fail regularly because we are severely limited by our humanity. It's easy to pick up an offense. We get trapped in jealousy. And most of us have trust issues that make loving others a huge challenge.

But God gives you the ability to love. When your faith is in the Lord as your Provider, you'll learn to love with passion and purpose because of His help.

54

He Knows Your Needs

"Therefore, don't worry and say, 'What are we going to eat?' or 'What are we going to drink?' or 'What are we going to wear?' Gentiles long for all these things. Your heavenly Father knows that you need them."
MATTHEW 6:31–32 CEB

Sometimes it feels impossible to not worry about our basic needs. These are the times our faith is challenged. This is when we waver in our belief. Why? Because we're afraid of losing what we hold dear. We worry about the future if we're unable to care for ourselves and our families in the most crucial ways.

Friend, God knows every need you have. Even more, He promises to take care of you. Every time you feel worried, ask the Lord to bless you with an unshakable faith in His trustworthiness. Ask God to remind you of His presence and promises. Then stand steadfast with expectation.

55

The Gifts

"After a long absence, the master of those three servants came back and settled up with them. The one given five thousand dollars showed him how he had doubled his investment. His master commended him: 'Good work! You did your job well. From now on be my partner.' "

MATTHEW 25:19–21 MSG

What will you do with the gifts God has given you? They weren't carelessly handed out. He didn't give everyone the same gift. Instead, God was thoughtful about what He would give each of us. He planned it out with precision, and His hope is that we will steward it well.

It takes courage and strength to follow the call God has placed on our life. It requires prayerful guidance. And it takes a willingness to choose His way over our way every day. The more time we invest in our relationship with God, the more unshakable our faith becomes, allowing us to bless Him with our gifts.

56

One True God

*I want you to know that the Eternal your God
is the only true God. He's the faithful God who
keeps His covenants and shows loyal love
for a thousand generations to those who in
return love Him and keep His commands.*

DEUTERONOMY 7:9 VOICE

There are many gods fighting for our time and attention. When we begin to worship something above the one true God, we are, by default, investing in false gods. These can be money, fame, stuff, status, or a myriad of other earthly offerings, but they all take our focus off the faithful God. They entice us to place our trust in the wrong things.

We can have immovable faith by keeping our eyes on God. We can let the things of this earth grow strangely dim by training our heart to long for Him alone. And we can use this time on earth to honor the Lord with our life.

57

Unshakable Kingdom

*Since we are receiving our rights to an
unshakable kingdom we should be extremely
thankful and offer God the purest worship
that delights his heart as we lay down our
lives in absolute surrender, filled with awe.*

HEBREWS 12:28 TPT

What a blessing to know that our eternal life will be celebrated in an unshakable kingdom. That means nothing can upset it or overturn it or undo it. And honestly, it's a gift to realize our time in heaven will be secure, because it's a stark contrast from the life we're living right now.

Where do you feel shaken the most right now? Is it in an important relationship? Maybe it's in your parenting skills or trying to navigate life with an elderly parent. Maybe your financial situation is destabilizing. Is it a change in your health? Friend, choose to anchor your faith in God now and live expectantly for His unshakable kingdom later.

58

Heavenly Cheering Section

*As for us, we have all of these great witnesses
who encircle us like clouds. So we must
let go of every wound that has pierced us
and the sin we so easily fall into. Then we
will be able to run life's marathon race with
passion and determination, for the path
has been already marked out before us.*

HEBREWS 12:1 TPT

You can do this. Whatever you're facing that's scary or intimidating, you can overcome it. Whatever is weighing you down, you can beat it. You may feel shaky right now, but when you lean on God, you're invincible.

Even more, you have a heavenly cheering section of those who've gone before you. They've experienced the faithfulness of God and run their race with passion and determination. They know He will give you necessary tools to finish well when you cling to Him. Since God is for you, who (or what) can be against you?

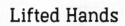

59

Lifted Hands

*So be made strong even in your weakness
by lifting up your tired hands in prayer and
worship. And strengthen your weak knees, for
as you keep walking forward on God's paths all
your stumbling ways will be divinely healed!*

HEBREWS 12:12–13 TPT

When you feel you have nothing left for the battle, scripture tells us to raise our "tired hands in prayer and worship." It may take all the strength we have, but this act of surrender changes things. The truth is we're all familiar with these moments of exhaustion. Maybe you're in one right now. So if that's you, let this prayer lead you into a deeper time with the Lord.

God's Word promises healing to our hearts when we continue to pursue the Lord, keeping our eyes on Him every day. He gives us hope for the future. It's not always easy, but it's always worth it! Only God can strengthen our faith through weakness.

60

He Hears Your Prayers

When you call me and come and pray to me,
I will listen to you. When you search for me, yes,
search for me with all your heart, you will find me.

JEREMIAH 29:12-13 CEB

Some people think God is elusive, but it's simply not true. He hears us. When we bow our heads and lift our voices in prayer, God listens. And when we seek Him wholeheartedly, He will be found. So if you are feeling distant from your Creator today, it's not on His end.

One of the smartest things we can do as believers is anchor our faith securely to God. He is the answer to every question we have. The Lord is the remedy for every ailment we suffer. He's the hope that holds us together. Let God be your first stop when difficulties arise, because He hears you and will reveal Himself in your situation.

61

He Knows the Plans

*"For I know the plans I have for you," says
the Eternal, "plans for peace, not evil, to give
you a future and hope—never forget that."*
JEREMIAH 29:11 VOICE

Sometimes we need a reminder that God is in control.
When everything feels chaotic, we need to trust that He
has the whole world in His hands. God very specifically
created plans for your future that are full of hope. He
wasn't in a bad mood when He designed your life. Even
knowing the trials and tribulations that would come your
way, God planned for peace and a hopeful heart to prevail.

That means you can experience unshakable faith
right now because you're a believer, trusting He has full
and complete knowledge in the details surrounding your
one and only life. God understands what's coming. And
when you pray to the Lord for help, He knows exactly
what you need.

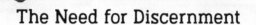

62

The Need for Discernment

*The LORD of heavenly forces, the God of Israel,
proclaims: Don't let the prophets and diviners in
your midst mislead you. Don't pay attention to
your dreams. They are prophesying lies to you in
my name. I didn't send them, declares the LORD.*
JEREMIAH 29:8–9 CEB

One of the things we should ask for as the faithful is discernment. We need to be able to cut through the issue to the core, knowing what's right and what's wrong. And because we have limitations as humans, we need God's supernatural and perfect discernment to flow through us.

Ask Him to help you discern the words of others. Ask for understanding, being able to distinguish lies from the truth. And in these last days, let the Holy Spirit prompt you to recognize incorrect doctrine or theology. When you ask God, He will sharpen your faith and anchor it in His truth.

63

All Day Long

LORD, listen closely to me and answer me,
because I am poor and in need. Guard my life
because I am faithful. Save your servant who
trusts in you—you! My God! Have mercy on me,
Lord, because I cry out to you all day long.

PSALM 86:1-3 CEB

Why do you think the psalmist cried out to God all day long? Was it because of his unshakable faith? The psalmist may not have known how God was going to help or when God was going to show up, but he believed He would. Friend, that takes a lot of faith to walk out.

Choose to have a persistent and patient faith. As a believer, you're blessed with unlimited access to God. That means you can cry out to Him as often as necessary. And you can rest assured that God will respond to you in His perfect timing and His perfect way.

64

The Wonder-Worker

My Lord! There is no one like you among the gods! There is nothing that can compare to your works! All the nations that you've made will come and bow down before you, Lord; they will glorify your name, because you are awesome and a wonder-worker. You are God. Just you.

PSALM 86:8–10 CEB

So often we feel small and insignificant compared to the challenges we face. We feel cornered by fear—boxed in by insecurities. Sometimes it seems we're left to our own devices as we try to navigate the muddy waters. But, friend, your God is a wonder-worker.

Anchor your faith in the truth that there's no one above Him, beside Him, or in front of Him. The Lord is incomparable in every way! Let this grow your faith to be rock solid. We serve a majestic and sovereign God who lavishes compassion on those who love Him.

65

A Teachable Spirit

*Teach me your way, LORD, so that I
can walk in your truth. Make my heart
focused only on honoring your name.*
PSALM 86:11 CEB

When your faith is secure in God, you will have a teachable spirit by default. You'll recognize the need for God's guidance in every area of your life, and you will seek it with fervor. Even more, your desire for the truth will enable you to walk it out daily.

So let the words you speak and the things you do point to your Father in heaven. Be intentional to focus your heart on honoring Him, and your obedience will yield beautiful blessings. Every day, ask God to show you the path He's determined for you to traverse. As you keep your eyes on the Lord and listen for His voice, you'll learn how to navigate the ups and downs of life with passion and purpose.

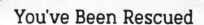

66

You've Been Rescued

*I give thanks to you, my Lord, my God, with
all my heart, and I will glorify your name
forever, because your faithful love toward
me is awesome and because you've rescued
my life from the lowest part of hell.*

PSALM 86:12–13 CEB

Friend, you have been rescued. Chances are you didn't even know you needed to be saved, but God pulled you from the depths of sin and redeemed your life through His Son, Jesus. Have you taken time to thank Him for the sacrifice and atonement?

Once we realize the depth of God's love, we are humbled. It makes us weak-kneed to know our Creator sees so much value in who we are that He reaches down and rescues us. That kind of love stabilizes our faith, deepening our dependence on God. And recognizing the lengths He's gone through to save us creates an immovable sense of appreciation and loyalty.

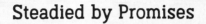

67

Steadied by Promises

*No one will be able to oppose you for as long
as you live. I will be with you just as I was with
Moses, and I will never fail or abandon you. . . .
Always be strong and courageous, and always
live by all of the law I gave to my servant Moses,
never turning from it—even ever so slightly—
so that you may succeed wherever you go.*

JOSHUA 1:5, 7 VOICE

What a powerful promise of protection and purpose! With such big shoes to fill, it's no wonder Joshua struggled with fear. Yes, God knew Joshua needed encouragement to anchor his faith.

Friend, let the same promises hold you steady too. What a privilege to have a God who is with us always. No matter what we're going through, no matter what we are facing, He is right there. Let that comfort your heart today and strengthen your faith as you take the next step.

With You Always

*This is My command: be strong and
courageous. Never be afraid or discouraged
because I am your God, the Eternal One, and
I will remain with you wherever you go.*

Joshua 1:9 voice

This is a tough command. As women, we struggle with all kinds of fear and discouragement. We get disheartened in our marriages. We worry for our kids as they begin to venture out from our protective bubble. We find ourselves anxious over finances and aging parents and an unstable job market. And when we look at the state of the world, it often makes us want to close the blinds and lock the doors.

But God is clear when He says our faith can be unshakable because He's with us wherever we go. It's becoming clearer that our only hope for peace is in the Lord. We really can live courageously by embracing the truth in today's verse.

69

The Perfection of God

*He's the Rock, and His work is perfect;
everything He does is right. He's the God
who can be trusted, who never does wrong
because He's righteous and upright.*

DEUTERONOMY 32:4 VOICE

What a beautiful and powerful definition of our heavenly Father. In a world full of so much darkness and evil, allow this truth to sink deep into your heart and encourage you. Let it give you hope that when you fasten your faith to the Lord, He will guide you into His goodness. When you choose to follow God, that decision will lead to blessing.

The world offers you many counterfeit gods to cling to. It makes magnificent promises in hopes of swaying your allegiance. But why choose anything over the perfection of God? If you want your faith to be unshakable and immovable when the storms hit, choose today to trust God above all else.

70

Demonstrating Faithful Love

My beloved friend, I commend you for your
demonstration of faithful love by all that you
have done for the brothers on their journey,
even though they were strangers at the time.

3 JOHN 5 TPT

Community is an important part of faith. God designed it to be a way of encouraging us to keep up the good fight. Oftentimes, friends and family are the ones who speak truth and wisdom when we need it the most. They are the ones who come alongside us in those hard moments and keep us steady. Be careful to not push aside the importance of people in your life.

Even more, be willing to demonstrate faithful love to others. If you see a need, meet a need. Open your heart and home when the Holy Spirit prompts you. And have the kind of steady faith that allows God to move you to action to accomplish His will.

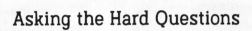

Asking the Hard Questions

This is how we have discovered love's reality:
Jesus sacrificed his life for us. Because
of this great love, we should be willing to
lay down our lives for one another.

1 JOHN 3:16 TPT

Oh boy. What is your response to today's verse? Chances are this willingness is fathomable when considering a mother. A mother would lay down her life for her children without question. We may feel that way about those close to us. But what's being asked is not that narrow. The idea is that our faithful love would mirror that of Jesus.

Meditate on this scripture today, and ask God to clarify what it looks like in your life. Ask for a courageous spirit. Have an honest conversation with the Lord, because unshakable faith enables you to ask hard questions. Wrestle it out through prayer and time in God's Word. And always remember His heart for you is always good. God delights in your steadfastness.

72

Self-Criticism

My dear children, let's not just talk about love;
let's practice real love. This is the only way
we'll know we're living truly, living in God's
reality. It's also the way to shut down debilitating
self-criticism, even when there is something to it.
For God is greater than our worried hearts and
knows more about us than we do ourselves.

1 John 3:18–20 msg

For many of us, self-criticism is a real issue that covers us in shame. We worry we're too big or too loud or too dumb. We look at others and compare our worst with their best. And it suffocates and weakens our faith because we feel unworthy of His love.

Take every one of those thoughts to God, and let Him create in you a confident faith that's unshakable. We don't have to be perfect to be loved. Our Creator knows us better than we know ourselves, and He finds us completely lovable.

73

You Are a Child of God

*What marvelous love the Father has
extended to us! Just look at it—we're called
children of God! That's who we really
are. But that's also why the world doesn't
recognize us or take us seriously, because
it has no idea who he is or what he's up to.*

1 JOHN 3:1 MSG

The world may not understand or appreciate God, but we do. They may think we're crazy for placing our faith in an invisible person, but we see His fingerprints all over our life. Don't be discouraged when your beliefs are mocked. Let not your heart be stressed when the world turns its back on God. No matter what, your faith can stand strong in the Father, who is alive and active every day.

Remember, you are called a child of God! You're loved and valued! Stand strong in that beautiful truth, and let His light shine through you.

74

Our Condemning Heart

*My delightfully loved friends, when our
hearts don't condemn us, we have a bold
freedom to speak face-to-face with God.*

1 JOHN 3:21 TPT

Shame is a terrible accuser. It lurks in the shadows and is always ready to whisper into our spirit that who we are is not good. Guilt says what we've *done* is wrong, but shame says *we* are wrong. And when we're embarrassed by our words or actions, knowing our choices dishonored God, we tend to turn from Him in humiliation.

It may take all the courage you can muster, but go to God when you feel ashamed. Don't sit in that sinking feeling, because nothing should interfere with the bold freedom you have to speak directly to Him. Be quick to confess your sins, removing any barrier that might interfere with your steadfast faith in God. And remember, He isn't expecting perfection from your life, just the pursuit of righteous living.

75

Unwavering Faith to Follow

So these are his commands: that we continually place our trust in the name of his Son, Jesus Christ, and that we keep loving one another, just as he has commanded us. For all who obey his commands find their lives joined in union with him, and he lives and flourishes in them.

1 JOHN 3:23-24 TPT

If asked, most would say they trust the Lord, almost like it's a no-brainer. But when the rubber meets the road, it's difficult to let go of the reins. Saying we trust God is a lot easier than actually trusting Him.

But there are powerful benefits to letting the Lord be in the driver's seat. Our obedience brings us into a deeper relationship with God. And we'll feel His strength and power working through us as we navigate the ups and downs of life. Ask God to give you unwavering faith to follow Him.

16

A Committed Faith

Therefore, submit to God. Resist the devil, and he will run away from you. Come near to God, and he will come near to you. Wash your hands, you sinners. Purify your hearts, you double-minded.

JAMES 4:7–8 CEB

Surrendering to God takes a bold faith that chooses to believe He is good and loving. It reveals a level of trust that comes from life experiences and time in the Word. Following behind the Lord as He leads proves a heart submitted to the Father and His ways.

God delights in your obedience, friend. He sees the sacrifices you make every day to do His will. The Lord recognizes the struggles you wrestle with as you set aside your fleshly desires and invest in His eternal ones instead. And every *yes* you give God matters greatly. So choose to have a committed faith that glorifies His unmatched magnificence and sovereignty.

11

Our Unchanging God

*Jesus, the Anointed One, is always the
same—yesterday, today, and forever.*

HEBREWS 13:8 TPT

For many, this is one of the most comforting verses in the
entire Bible because it reminds us that God is unchanging.
No matter what happens, we can count on His consistency. The God of yesterday is the God of today and will
be the same all-powerful God of tomorrow. His mood
is unaffected by the ups and downs of humanity, and
His love is unfailingly dependable. The Lord's steadiness
is why our faith can be unshakable.

Change can be destabilizing for many of us, so let this
powerful truth anchor your faith and secure your heart to
the Father. In this world, you'll experience ebbs and flows,
and there's no way to stop it. Relationships will come and
go. Parenting seasons will change. But as a believer, you
can cling to God for stability and peace through it all.

78

Hitting Rock Bottom

*Quit playing the field. Hit bottom, and
cry your eyes out. The fun and games
are over. Get serious, really serious. Get
down on your knees before the Master;
it's the only way you'll get on your feet.*

JAMES 4:9-10 MSG

There's something to be said about the necessity of hitting
rock bottom. So often, that's exactly what must happen
before we will bend our knee and look up to our God.
Until we're at the end of ourselves, we'll continue trying to
claw and scrape our way out of the pit in our own strength.

This powerful place of surrender is where God becomes very real. It's here we realize our desperate need
for Him. This is where we release control and hold on to
the Lord for dear life. Even more, it's also where we find
our footing, giving us a firm foundation of faith to stand on.

79

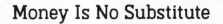

Money Is No Substitute

*Don't be obsessed with money but live
content with what you have, for you always
have God's presence. For hasn't he promised
you, "I will never leave you, never! And I
will not loosen my grip on your life!"*

HEBREWS 13:5 TPT

When we become obsessed with money, it removes the need for God. It gives us a false sense of security, thinking we can buy our way out of any trouble. Money becomes a god of sorts and helps us feel empowered to navigate the ups and downs of life on our own. But that mindset will bite us in the end.

Scripture is quick to remind us that our contentment and security come from God's presence alone. Anytime we try to substitute worldly offerings for Him, we'll be disappointed. Friend, there's nothing more powerful than God manifesting in your life. That's why we can stand strong in faith and weather every storm.

80

God Is for You

So we can say with great confidence: "I know the Lord is for me and I will never be afraid of what people may do to me!" Don't forget the example of your spiritual leaders who have spoken God's messages to you, take a close look at how their lives ended, and then follow their walk of faith.

HEBREWS 13:6–7 TPT

Fear is a tool of the enemy, used to undermine our belief in the Lord. If allowed, it would consume us. But consider that God combats it with community. He's placed faith-filled people in your life for a reason. Watching their unshakable faith helps create the same in you. And they'll remind you that God's goodness is always at work.

Friend, God is always in your corner. Even when you can't see Him in your circumstances, don't waver in your trust. Remember, He's always for you, so there is nothing to fear.

81

Powerful Protector

*Pray also that we would all be rescued from
the snares of harmful, wicked people—after
all, not all people are believing. Still, the
Lord is true to His promises; He will hold you
up and guard you against the evil one.*

2 Thessalonians 3:2–3 voice

God is true to His promises. If scripture says He'll stand guard, keeping you from the enemy's grip, He will do so. When your faith is activated and steadfast, you'll see mighty moves of the Lord in your circumstances because you will recognize His hand moving. You'll see His protection from the wicked intentions of others. And it will strengthen your believing heart like nothing else.

Let daily prayer for His covering become a habit. Ask for an increased measure of faith to know His promises are true. And lean into God over anything and anyone else because He is your powerful Protector. . .forever.

82

Whole and Holy

*May God himself, the God who makes
everything holy and whole, make you holy
and whole, put you together—spirit, soul, and
body—and keep you fit for the coming of our
Master, Jesus Christ. The One who called you is
completely dependable. If he said it, he'll do it!*

1 Thessalonians 5:23-24 msg

Here's what's so beautiful about today's scripture reading. It solidifies the truth that it's God—not you—who makes you whole and holy. Too often we put the pressure on ourselves to become something we cannot become without God's intervention. We can work hard to pursue righteous living, but we'll fail if He's not a part of the process.

While the world tells you to be an independent woman, faith says to depend on God. It's the Lord who makes you righteous and acceptable. So attach your faith to our loyal and steadfast God, who is true to His Word!

83

Mentorship

*And now, beloved brothers and sisters, since
you have been mentored by us with respect
to living for God and pleasing him, I appeal
to you in the name of the Lord Jesus with
this request: keep faithfully growing through
our teachings even more and more.*

1 THESSALONIANS 4:1 TPT

We've all been mentored by somebody. There have been people placed in our lives to help challenge and grow our faith to where it is today. Chances are we've even had those who have been instrumental in encouraging us from afar who don't even know we exist. Let's recognize the beauty of believers who have helped mature our faith to where it is today.

And now that we've found our footing and our faith has taken root and is secure in the love of God, it's important we continue to grow. One day you may be the mentor someone else needs.

84

Comforting Others through Suffering

He always comes alongside us to comfort us in every suffering so that we can come alongside those who are in any painful trial. We can bring them this same comfort that God has poured out upon us.

2 Corinthians 1:4 tpt

Consider that your season of suffering has a greater purpose than you may imagine. Maybe one of the reasons you had the privilege of walking through it was so you could help others navigate their own season of suffering. Few things encourage a heart more than knowing someone has been through the fire and lived to tell the story. Friend, you have the opportunity to bring comfort to a weary soul.

Thank God for creating in you an unshakable faith that allows you to help create that faith in others. How wonderful to realize your difficulties have a higher purpose! Community is a powerful tool that brings unexpected and beautiful blessings!

85

The Craving of Comfort

*If troubles weigh us down, that just means
that we will receive even more comfort to
pass on to you for your deliverance! For
the comfort pouring into us empowers us to
bring comfort to you. And with this comfort
upholding you, you can endure victoriously
the same suffering that we experience.*

2 CORINTHIANS 1:6 TPT

Where do you find comfort in this world? Is your spouse the one you look to? Maybe it's retail therapy or a huge bowl of ice cream. Do you feel reassured by numbing out with substances or bingeing Netflix? Because of this broken world, we all have good reasons to crave comfort and kindness. It's something we all want, something we all need, but unless we're going to the Source, any comfort we feel will be short-lived and leave us in want.

Friend, anchor your faith in God so He can be your everything and meet your every need.

Drawing Heaven's Attention

Because there are so many interceding for us,
our deliverance will cause even more people
to give thanks to God. What a gracious gift of
mercy surrounds us because of your prayers!

2 Corinthians 1:11 TPT

Never pass up an opportunity to ask for prayer or to be a prayer partner for others. Intercession plays a key role in our liberation because it draws heaven's attention to our earthly battles. It's a powerful weapon in our arsenal of faith.

In addition, consider there are those watching your life because they know you're a follower of Jesus. They look to you for guidance as they walk out their circumstances, whether you realize it or not. So let your deliverance be transparent so others can find encouragement and hope as they wait for their own. And watch how your faith strengthens through intercessory prayer and how the faith of others strengthens through your deliverance.

87

Constantly Strengthening

Now, it is God himself who has anointed us. And he is constantly strengthening both you and us in union with Christ.

2 CORINTHIANS 1:21 TPT

Where does your strength come from? For many of us, we might proudly point to ourselves. We may brag it's been passed down through generations of women in our family. We might attribute it to making it through tough life experiences or finding a balance through meditation. But the truth is our strength comes from God Himself. When we give credit to anyone or anything else, our faith is unsteady.

And not only does He strengthen you in the battle, but it's a continual strengthening that doesn't stop. It's an ongoing renewal that helps you stand strong as the battle rages. Your prayerfulness and obedience unlock God's blessing in beautiful ways. That kind of unshakable faith allows Him room to intervene on your behalf.

88

His Seal of Love

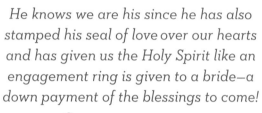

*He knows we are his since he has also
stamped his seal of love over our hearts
and has given us the Holy Spirit like an
engagement ring is given to a bride—a
down payment of the blessings to come!*

2 CORINTHIANS 1:22 TPT

Because they are yours, you could find your kids in a crowd in seconds flat. You know their silhouette. You could home in on the direction of their voices. Why? Because they are connected to you in meaningful ways. You know their faces, their mannerisms, and their inflections as they speak.

God knows you completely. Even more, scripture says He's stamped His seal of love over your heart and filled it with the Holy Spirit as a down payment. And even as miraculous as this is, it's only a down payment! Let your faith be steadied as you realize you are marked by your Creator!

89

Your Temple

Don't you know that your body is the temple
of the Holy Spirit who comes from God and
dwells inside of you? You do not own yourself.
You have been purchased at a great price,
so use your body to bring glory to God!
1 CORINTHIANS 6:19–20 VOICE

Friend, let this verse help you gain the right perspective when it comes to seeing your body as a temple. God's Spirit dwells in you because Jesus' death on the cross paid the ransom for your sins, making you right with God. And because you've been redeemed, your body—your life—should be focused on bringing glory to God.

Cling to this beautiful truth every day. The world will try to sow seeds of division in your heart, hoping you will make the wrong choices with how you live. Be resolute to keep your faith in God steadfast and unwavering—body, soul, and spirit.

90

Renewing Your Mind

*Don't be conformed to the patterns of this world,
but be transformed by the renewing of your
minds so that you can figure out what God's
will is—what is good and pleasing and mature.*
ROMANS 12:2 CEB

Only when your mind is renewed through faith in God will you be able to discern His will for your life. This renewal is a daily choice you make to engage with the Father, inviting Him to transform your mind from worldly thoughts to eternal ones. And while God is the only One who can facilitate this beautiful change, it's your steadfast faith that leads to surrender, opening the door to His goodness.

The desire of your heart should be to know God more each day so your faith will grow and mature. Ask Him to renew your mind so you can recognize the perfect path He's carved out for you to follow.

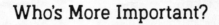

Who's More Important?

Because of the grace allotted to me, I can respectfully tell you not to think of yourselves as being more important than you are; devote your minds to sound judgment since God has assigned to each of us a measure of faith.

ROMANS 12:3 VOICE

If you are hyper-focused on your importance in the world, you're placing yourself above God. The reality is most of us are overly concerned with having our needs met. We're obsessed with the burdens we are carrying and how they affect our heart. Many of us live offended and focus on all the wrong coming our way. And without realizing it, our thoughts and actions reveal the problem. Our faithfulness has been replaced by our selfishness.

Take every struggle, fear, and insecurity to God. Let Him strengthen your faith and renew your hope as you trust for divine solutions. And keep your eyes on His importance over yours.

92

From the Center

Love from the center of who you are; don't fake it. Run for dear life from evil; hold on for dear life to good. Be good friends who love deeply; practice playing second fiddle.
ROMANS 12:9–10 MSG

At the very center of you is your God-determined identity. That's why scripture says to love from the center of yourself, because it's the most honest and real place. Most of us struggle to do so because we've been hurt in the past. We've shared our heart, and it has bitten us in the backside. So to protect our fragility, we've created a fake persona that feels more acceptable to the world.

Ask God to heal that wound and untangle your worth. Turn from the evil lies and messages you've internalized. Surround yourself with friends you can love from the center. And through prayer and time in God's Word, let your faith in His provision and love become unshakable.

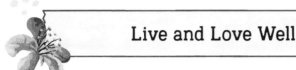

93

Live and Love Well

Bless your enemies; no cursing under your breath. Laugh with your happy friends when they're happy; share tears when they're down. Get along with each other; don't be stuck-up. Make friends with nobodies; don't be the great somebody.

ROMANS 12:14-16 MSG

Today's passage is a challenge to every believer to live and love well. Some may think it's common sense and that they don't need a refresher course, but if we all followed its commands, the world would be a kinder place. And while some may think living this way is easy, it actually takes a great deal of faith to walk it out with consistency.

Don't be quick to dismiss today's verses. Instead, ask God to reveal where you're falling short, and then commit to following each one with passion and purpose, trusting the Lord to anchor your feet and your faith in His will.

94

Living in Peace

Don't hit back; discover beauty in everyone. If you've got it in you, get along with everybody. Don't insist on getting even; that's not for you to do. "I'll do the judging," says God. "I'll take care of it."

ROMANS 12:17–19 MSG

Peace matters to God. It's a fruit of the Spirit He promises to grow and mature in us. Even more, God directly asks for believers to find ways to get along and live peacefully whenever possible. How can we? By deepening our relationship with the Lord daily and asking for a heart of reconciliation and harmony.

When we choose to obey God, He promises to exact justice on our behalf. He'll judge. He'll take care of things. And this beautiful promise frees us from feeling the need for revenge. Let God be your strong tower, and let faith settle your spirit with His comfort.

95

Contentment

*Be happy in your hope, stand your ground when
you're in trouble, and devote yourselves to prayer.*
ROMANS 12:12 CEB

These three things take discipline and intentionality. You can't live this way if you're on autopilot. You can't be in shutdown mode, hoping things will just work themselves out. You must have clear eyes and a clear head to be effective, and your heart must be full of unshakable faith for these to be active in your life.

Listen, friend, your relationship with God is the most important relationship you will ever have. From it comes the ability to live with courage and confidence, strength and power, and wisdom and discernment. You can be happy. You can dare to hope. You can stand your ground. And when you devote yourself to prayer, being honest with God about the state of your heart, you can find contentment even in the most difficult times.

96

Since God Stands with Us

So, what does all this mean? If God has determined to stand with us, tell me, who then could ever stand against us?

ROMANS 8:31 TPT

We've all felt the hurt from being picked on or ganged up on by others. We've been the target of evil motives and careless actions. Chances are our name and reputation have been dragged through the dirt more than once. And we've heard the horrible things said behind our back. But today's verse reminds us of one very important truth: we have God on our side, and that trumps anything or anyone who tries to come against us.

When our faith in the Lord is securely anchored and immovable, we'll have a supernatural perspective on life. We'll see the bigger picture. We won't major on the minors. And our hearts will be steadied knowing God is right here, standing with us.

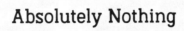

Absolutely Nothing

*So who can separate us? What can come
between us and the love of God's Anointed?
Can troubles, hardships, persecution,
hunger, poverty, danger, or even death?
The answer is, absolutely nothing.*

ROMANS 8:35 VOICE

We're conditioned to have relational chaos and breakdown. We expect difficult seasons. We recognize the reality of separation and divorce. And we are rarely surprised when something comes between us and those we care about. It's just part of life, right? Although it's painful, we've had no choice but to find ways to navigate it time and time again.

What a refreshing revelation to know nothing can separate us from God's love. It simply can't happen. And it's hard to accept this as truth because we're used to heartbreak, abandonment, rejection, and irreconcilable differences. But God is clear in His Word when He says absolutely nothing can separate us from His love. Ask God for confident faith to live, believing this promise!

98

The Holy Spirit

In a similar way, the Holy Spirit takes hold of us in our human frailty to empower us in our weakness. For example, at times we don't even know how to pray, or know the best things to ask for. But the Holy Spirit rises up within us to super-intercede on our behalf, pleading to God with emotional sighs too deep for words.

ROMANS 8:26 TPT

If you're a believer, you can have unshakable faith knowing your needs are supernaturally made known to God. Even if you can't express yourself, the Holy Spirit intercedes on your behalf. Every heartache is fully understood by Him. God knows every detail. And when you forget to pray, the Spirit is already pleading with God.

The Holy Spirit plays an important role in every believer's life. One of the most significant ways is by advocating for us through prayer when we can't find the words ourselves.

99

Weaving Together for Good

So we are convinced that every detail of our lives is continually woven together for good, for we are his lovers who have been called to fulfill his designed purpose.

ROMANS 8:28 TPT

Can you imagine the attention to detail it would take for this verse to be true? Think of the complexity and intricacies involved! So let's consider it a powerful blessing that no matter what we're facing—be it the good times, the hard times, or the broken times—God in His sovereignty weaves them together for good.

The next time your life feels overwhelming or bad news blankets your heart, remember God will use it all to benefit you. It may make no sense on the front end. There may be nothing positive in sight. You may be full of anger and sadness. But you can stand strong on His promises, including the one from today's scripture.

100

The Blessing of Standing Strong

If you abide in Me and My voice abides in you,
anything you ask will come to pass for you.
Your abundant growth and your faithfulness
as My followers will bring glory to the Father.

JOHN 15:7-8 VOICE

God is asking you to stand strong in your faith. He wants your belief in His power and might to be unwavering. In a world that builds its foundation on shifting sand, God is asking you to let His voice be what guides you instead. He recognizes the tug-of-war between the world's way and His way and understands the tension it brings. And so God makes a promise.

Friend, your choice to have unshakable faith will bring blessings your way. So follow His commands and listen for His voice. When you do, you will reap the rewards through answered prayer. Even more, your faith will glorify His name.

101

The State of Your Faith

Many leaders secretly believed in Him
but would not declare their faith because
the Pharisees continued their threats to
expel all His followers from the synagogue;
here's why: they loved to please men more
than they desired to glorify God.

JOHN 12:42-43 VOICE

Do you hide your faith because you worry it might ruin your reputation? Do you downplay your involvement in church to avoid being judged? Do you praise God in private but ignore Him in public? Be careful. These are hard questions to answer, but they shine the proverbial spotlight on the state of your faith. Is it steadfast or wavering?

A steadfast faith in God is evident by its consistency. Be it in good times or in bad, in public or in private, in joy or sadness, it's anchored in the Lord's provision and love. Ask God for revelation of your own faith, and then follow His lead from there.

102

Nothing Is Impossible

Jesus said to him, "Get up! Pick up your mat and walk." Immediately the man was well, and he picked up his mat and walked. Now that day was the Sabbath.
JOHN 5:8–9 CEB

Think of the faith this crippled man displayed in this moment. His life had been limited to a mat. While we don't know his whole story, chances are he'd seen doctors with no hope of healing. He had made peace with his situation because he had no other options. But when Jesus commanded him to stand up, he obeyed right away and received a blessing for it.

Let this encourage you to trust God with your whole heart and follow His ways. The Lord has power and dominion over every human limitation. What you need may seem impossible. Your heart's desire may look impossible. But with God, nothing is impossible. Believing this will guarantee unshakable faith.

103

Fear Is Not from God

*God will never give you the spirit of
fear, but the Holy Spirit who gives you
mighty power, love, and self-control.*
2 TIMOTHY 1:7 TPT

Remember that anytime you feel fear, it is not from God. When you're worried about the future or afraid for the upcoming hard conversation or scared about your doctor's appointment, the Lord isn't the source. So anytime your anxiety creeps in, let it be a red flag that your once unshakable faith is now. . .shaky at best.

God loves us too much to give us the spirit of fear. He came to empower us through our belief in Him to live with passion and purpose. His Spirit gives us the power to do so. In addition, God blessed us with an abundant measure of love and self-control. These three work in harmony to build our faith and help us walk out our calling.

104

Be a Light

Keep your eyes open, hold tight to your convictions, give it all you've got, be resolute, and love without stopping.
1 CORINTHIANS 16:13–14 MSG

This is a call to have bold faith! In a world that often brings so much sadness and suffering, by faith we're able to find joy regardless. Even when it looks dark and hopeless in every direction, through God we can love others in meaningful ways. The world can't beat us, because He has overcome it!

But it's important to also be vigilant, keeping our eyes open as we cling tightly to our convictions. It's vital we're unbendable in our belief of who God is and what He promises to do. We can't become lazy in our faith, expecting God to pick up the slack. Instead, let's guard our heart against the enemy's schemes. Let your steadfast faith be a light pointing others to your Father in heaven.

105

An Expectant Heart

Here's what I've learned through it all: Don't give up; don't be impatient; be entwined as one with the Lord. Be brave and courageous, and never lose hope. Yes, keep on waiting— for he will never disappoint you!

PSALM 27:14 TPT

Learning to wait on God can be grueling. Sometimes our patience runs thin, and we want immediate action to remedy the pain we're feeling. There are times we feel boxed in on every side, desperate for an escape route. But God asks us to be brave as we wait for answers to come.

Those with a strong resolve won't lose hope, because our eyes are focused on God's promises. We may not know when or how He'll show up, but our heart is expectant because our faith is unshakable. We believe God's Word when it says we won't be disappointed. And even more, we've personally witnessed His faithfulness time and time again.

106

Holds Your Feet Firmly

So don't turn your face away from me. You're the God of my salvation; how can you reject your servant in anger? You've been my only hope, so don't forsake me now when I need you!

PSALM 27:9 TPT

I'm sure you can remember times you felt this kind of desperation. Maybe your marriage was falling apart, or your child was the victim of trauma. Maybe you made a terrible decision that held unfathomable consequences. Maybe the worst scenario imaginable came true in your life. And you vacillated between being angry at God and worried God was angry at you. These are chaotic times emotionally and spiritually.

Unshakable faith matters because it holds your feet firmly to the ground when life spins out of control. It keeps you from worrying about what God thinks of you. It comforts your anxious heart because you know God loves you and is for you.

Day of Trouble

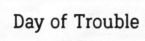

*In the day of trouble, he will treasure me in
his shelter, under the cover of his tent. He
will lift me high upon a rock, out of reach
from all my enemies who surround me.
Triumphant now, I'll bring him my offerings
of praise, singing and shouting with ecstatic
joy! Yes, I will sing praises to Yahweh!*

PSALM 27:5-6 TPT

What does your day of trouble look like? A pink slip at work? Divorce papers on the kitchen table? Foreclosure documents at your door? A betrayal exposed? The loss of a loved one? Everyone will face difficult moments where our only comfort will be God. Even with well-meaning friends and family standing in the gap, our soul will cry out for our Creator.

There is nothing more important in life than your relationship with God. Time spent in prayer and in the Word will be what anchors you in the storm. Invest well.

108

Because of Righteousness

*Guilty criminals experience paranoia even
though no one threatens them. But the innocent
lovers of God, because of righteousness, will
have the boldness of a young, ferocious lion!*

PROVERBS 28:1 TPT

Righteousness simply means living in a right relationship with God. How do you do that? The Bible is full of commands telling you God's desire for your life. The Word says we're to pray without ceasing. He wants us to forgive the unforgivable and love the unlovable. We're to exhibit the fruit of the Spirit. But today's verse also tells you why we're to live righteously.

When we're deeply connected with God, following His will and ways with purpose, we will enjoy a confident and steadfast faith. Scripture says we will be bold as lions, unwilling to give in to fear. We'll be ready to face every day courageously, trusting God even when heavy in battle. And we will stand tall because we lived right.

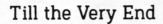

Till the Very End

Be strong, courageous, and effective. Do not fear or be dismayed. I know that the Eternal God, who is my God, is with you. He will not abandon you or forsake you until you have finished all the work for the temple of the Eternal.

1 CHRONICLES 28:20 VOICE

It takes perseverance to complete something. Some don't even know where to begin. They become paralyzed by anxiety and don't even start. Many get messed up in the middle because that's where the confusion often sets in, and they quit. And others get tripped up at the end. The journey has been long, and they're exhausted, and they wave the white flag before they ever cross the finish line.

As a woman of faith, God believes in you. He is with you. He wants you to be strong, courageous, and effective, knowing He'll be with you to the very end.

110

When God Is Your Everything

*You are my rock and my fortress—my
soul's sanctuary! Therefore, for the sake of
Your reputation, be my leader, my guide,
my navigator, my commander. Save me
from the snare that has been secretly set
out for me, for You are my protection.*

PSALM 31:3-4 VOICE

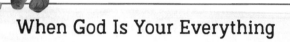

Unshakable faith knows God is our everything. It knows God is our protector and our strong tower. It knows He is the One who will lead us through the valley of the shadow of death. When our faith is unyielding, it enables us to find new confidence in God's ability. We simply believe He will fulfill every promise made. And it encourages a surrendered heart full of humility.

But the only way to have unshakable faith is through prayer and time in His Word. There is no substitute. There's no quick option. So choose every day to invest your time and your heart, knowing God is your everything.

III

All Things

I can do all things [which He has called me to do] through Him who strengthens and empowers me [to fulfill His purpose—I am self-sufficient in Christ's sufficiency; I am ready for anything and equal to anything through Him who infuses me with inner strength and confident peace.]

PHILIPPIANS 4:13 AMP

We can have confident faith in His plan, knowing if God called us to it, He'll equip us for it. You don't have to wonder if you're able. You don't have to worry about falling short. When you trust God to meet your needs, He will strengthen and empower you to fulfill every purpose. It might be a bumpy ride, but you'll find victory through Him.

Let's praise God for the promise to fill in the gap and make up the difference between our limitations and the plans He's established. Your job is obedience, believing He will come through every time you feel lacking.

112

Keep on Believing

Overhearing but ignoring what they said,
Jesus said to the ruler of the synagogue,
Do not be seized with alarm and struck
with fear; only keep on believing.
MARK 5:36 AMPC

Maybe the antidote to fear really is faith. When we choose to keep on believing in God rather than buying into what's trying to intimidate, we will find a place of peace. Fear requires our constant attention to thrive. When we don't focus on it, it loses power. When we do focus on it, we're consumed with horrible outcomes and endings.

Choose today to be a woman with unshakable faith. Decide right now that when fear begins to creep in, you'll take it right to God. You will shut it down. And instead of entertaining what scares you, focus on the goodness of God and all the ways He is blessing your life.

113

Blessed by Relationship

*Be strong in the Lord [draw your strength from
Him and be empowered through your union with
Him] and in the power of His [boundless] might.*
EPHESIANS 6:10 AMP

The more you go to the gym, the stronger your body feels. The more you study, the better you do on your test. The more you practice your craft, the greater your skill becomes. So it makes sense that the deeper your relationship with God, the more you will be blessed by it.

No matter what you're facing today, you have unlimited access to God's strength because of your steadfast faith. He will empower you for the next step as you navigate each circumstance. If you need wisdom, God will give it. Need discernment? Ask Him. Desperate for comfort and peace? Tell Him. He's not a genie in a bottle, friend. Instead, He is a loving God ready to honor your faithfulness and obedience.

114

The State of Your Heart

So stand firm and hold your ground, HAVING TIGHTENED THE WIDE BAND OF TRUTH (personal integrity, moral courage) AROUND YOUR WAIST and HAVING PUT ON THE BREASTPLATE OF RIGHTEOUSNESS (an upright heart).

Ephesians 6:14 AMP

In the battles you face, the state of your heart is very important. And God knows the value it brings when it's deeply rooted in faith. So when He tells you to stand firm and hold your ground, He knows it's doable because His heavenly armor and the benefits it brings are available to you. So every day, ask for their covering.

God's "band of truth" fitted around your waist enables integrity and moral courage. His "breastplate of righteousness" protects your heart, keeping it honorable and principled. Consider the advantage this will afford you in any situation! And recognize that your firm faith allows you access to these anytime you need them.

115

The Importance of Praying

Pray passionately in the Spirit, as you constantly intercede with every form of prayer at all times. Pray the blessings of God upon all his believers.

EPHESIANS 6:18 TPT

If you've ever wondered if prayer is important, reread today's verse. It could not be clearer, revealing the *how*, *when*, and *why* it's an important weapon in the believer's arsenal. God wants us to pray with all kinds of prayers and ask for everything we need. Nothing is off limits. And while we may not always get the answer we want, God will always answer in the ways we need.

Being a faithful woman of prayer means you must always be ready to intercede. Not only should you be praying for your own needs but also praying for all of God's people. Pray big and pray small. Pray locally, nationally, and all around the globe. But be unwavering in your prayer life!

116

Keeping Us from Fear

He will not fear bad news; his heart is
steadfast, trusting [confidently relying
on and believing] in the LORD.
PSALM 112:7 AMP

When your faith is steadfast, beautiful things happen. It changes everything because you're no longer operating in your own strength but instead acquiring it from the Father. And we can agree His ways are better than ours. So when we choose to trust God above all else, it reveals an unshakable confidence in His promises. It keeps us from fear, anxiety, and stress.

Today, ask the Lord to create in you a faith that never wavers. Let Him steady your anxious heart with peace and comfort. And when fear comes knocking on your door, turn from it and open your Bible. Drop to your knees and pray. Grow your faith muscle into a powerful companion. It's only through God that we will find strength to stand in the storms.

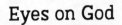

117

Eyes on God

*"Do not yield to fear, for I am always near.
Never turn your gaze from me, for I am your
faithful God. I will infuse you with my strength
and help you in every situation. I will hold
you firmly with my victorious right hand."*

ISAIAH 41:10 TPT

The moment we turn our gaze from God, things go wrong. Remember the faith of Peter stepping out of the boat and walking on water toward Jesus, only to sink once he looked down? Faith requires us to keep our eyes on God. It doesn't work any other way. But it also requires a humility many of us struggle to find.

It may not be a willful disobedience but rather a habit acquired over time. For whatever reason, we've learned to rely on ourselves, collecting an arsenal of worldly offerings to numb the fear and pain. Let God hold you firmly instead. He'll make your faith unshakable.

Consistent Faith

*The wise counsel GOD gives when I'm
awake is confirmed by my sleeping heart.
Day and night I'll stick with GOD; I've got
a good thing going and I'm not letting go.*
PSALM 16:7–8 MSG

Steadfast faith isn't a part-time job. It's not interchangeable based on your circumstances. It isn't inconsistent, because to be so would cause it to lose power. It never ebbs and flows with your feelings or emotions. Instead, steadfast faith is displayed day and night. You can see it in the good times and in the bad. And even when you can't see a way out, you stick with God because you believe He loves you and is for you.

The key to living and loving well is staying connected to the Lord no matter what. Ask for a fresh perspective to remind you why your connection to Him makes all the difference. And then commit your heart to consistent faith.

119

Run to God

*Keep me safe, O God, I've run for dear
life to you. I say to GOD, "Be my Lord!"
Without you, nothing makes sense.*
PSALM 16:1-2 MSG

Have you considered the safest place for you to be is in the presence of God? Too often, we look to the world to bring us a sense of security. We trust in all the wrong things, hoping something will bring the much-needed relief we're desperate for. But the psalmist understands the gravity of faith and how it anchors you securely to God when life feels chaotic. Do you?

Be the kind of woman who runs to God the moment things get messy. Let prayer be your first stop. And in that prayer time, praise Him on the front end for all the ways He's going to straighten your path. Pray with a confident, steadfast heart, knowing God is on the move!

120

Privileges

Yahweh, you alone are my inheritance.
You are my prize, my pleasure, and my
portion. You hold my destiny and its timing
in your hands. Your pleasant path leads me
to pleasant places. I'm overwhelmed by the
privileges that come with following you!

PSALM 16:5-6 TPT

There are powerful and abundant privileges that come from following God. Never think for a moment He is small. His promises don't fall flat. Instead, scripture makes clear that He is our everything. God is the answer to every question we have. And when we anchor our faith in Him, our path will lead to pleasant places.

What keeps you from fully trusting and following the Lord? Is it a stubborn streak? A prideful heart? Fear of giving up control? Learned behavior? Friend, humble yourself, asking God to open your eyes to His magnificence. Ask Him to steady your faith, and He will.

121

Wise and Innocent

*Behold, I am sending you out like sheep
in the midst of wolves; be wary and wise
as serpents, and be innocent (harmless,
guileless, and without falsity) as doves.*
MATTHEW 10:16 AMPC

It takes faith to walk out what today's verse is describing. It's important we remember that anything God asks of us comes with His help. He understands our ability to be wise comes from trusting for it. We can be innocent as doves because the Lord gives us the heart and mind so it can manifest in our life. The expectation isn't for us to figure things out. The expectation is to anchor our faith in Him.

Let God be the One to build your faith so it's unshakable every day, giving you the skills to follow His plan. Let Him be the One who fills you with wisdom and innocence for the purposes He's determined. God will always give you what you need.

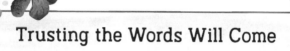

122

Trusting the Words Will Come

"So when they arrest you, don't worry about how to speak or what you are to say, for the Holy Spirit will give you at that very moment the words to speak. It won't be you speaking but the Spirit of your Father speaking through you."

MATTHEW 10:19–20 TPT

What a relief to know God will give the right words at the right time. Too often we get tongue-tied when we're desperate to speak with clarity. We forget what we wanted to say, or it comes out wrong. And rather than speak with power and authority, we lose the opportunity.

God is asking you to trust. He understands the seriousness of certain situations and what your heart is burdened to share. When you believe the Holy Spirit is aware and active, you can rest knowing He'll bring forth what needs to be spoken. You can trust the Spirit to speak through you.

123

Not Alarmed

The Eternal is my light amidst my darkness and my rescue in times of trouble. So whom shall I fear? He surrounds me with a fortress of protection. So nothing should cause me alarm.

PSALM 27:1 VOICE

What are the situations causing you alarm these days? Is there a health issue worrying you? Are you dealing with aging parents? Are your workplace conditions deteriorating? Is an important relationship strained? Or does the state of the world have you in a state of anxiety, feeling hopeless and scared? Friend, your only hope for lasting peace is found in the Lord's presence.

Let Him be your fortress of protection. Let God rescue you in moments that feel overwhelming. When you choose to surround yourself with His goodness rather than any worldly offering, your faith will become unshakable. Nothing will have the power to cause you alarm because you'll know you're safe.

124

Worst-Case Scenarios

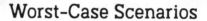

When my enemies advanced to devour me alive, they tripped and fell flat on their faces into the soil. When the armies of the enemy surround me, I will not be afraid. When death calls for me in the midst of war, my soul is confident and unmoved.

PSALM 27:2-3 VOICE

The psalmist is describing worst-case scenarios—adversaries advancing, being surrounded by the enemy, and the calling of death. To anyone, these would look like hopeless circumstances. But not when your faith is secured in God. When He is your anchor, your soul will be unmoved and unafraid.

Spend time talking to God today about the worst-case scenarios you are facing. Be honest about the places you feel surrounded by evil. Where are you clinging to hope with all your might? Friend, it's time to turn to the Lord and let Him be your stronghold, giving you a calm confidence in His love and loyalty.

125

The Reason We Choose to Wait

*But those who wait for Yahweh's grace will
experience divine strength. They will rise
up on soaring wings and fly like eagles,
run their race without growing weary,
and walk through life without giving up.*

ISAIAH 40:31 TPT

The key that unlocks God's grace and strength is *waiting*; and honestly, it's one of the hardest commands possible because we're programmed to want things to happen now. We make reservations and look for overnight shipping, same-day service, and microwavable food. Anything that causes a delay annoys and angers us. The truth is we have a waiting problem. Amen?

But as we look at the benefits that come from waiting, we discover a compelling argument for unshakable faith. Scripture says we'll navigate those difficult situations without growing weary. We'll find stamina for the journey. And through God's divine disbursement, our heart won't be overwhelmed but will persevere instead.

126

Timeless Promises

"The grass withers, the flower fades when the breath of Yahweh blows upon it; the people are just like grass! But even though grass withers and the flower fades, the word of our God stands strong forever!"

ISAIAH 40:7-8 TPT

It's a great comfort knowing God's Word will stand strong forever. It's unchangeable. It's irrefutable. It's immutable. And while everything and everyone else in the world are guaranteed to fade and wither over time, His promises won't. They never will. Friend, that truth is why your faith can be steadfast. God is the same today as He was yesterday, and He will remain the same tomorrow and beyond.

Don't be tricked into trusting anything other than the Lord. The world has nothing for you, and it cannot save you. If you are looking for hope, dig into God's Word and let it encourage and challenge you. His timeless promises are good for the heart!

127

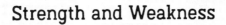

Strength and Weakness

He will care for you as a shepherd tends his flock, gathering the weak lambs and taking them in his arms. He carries them close to his heart and gently leads those that have young.

ISAIAH 40:11 TPT

There's a premium placed on being a strong woman. Society rewards those with unmatched strength, giving them "rock star" status. But this inadvertently causes us to stay silent when we feel weak. We don't want to be seen as a burden or ineffective. We don't want to feel *less than* others. We don't want our confidence to wane.

But in God's kingdom, weakness is not something negative. As a matter of fact, our weakness is an opportunity to be gathered up in His arms and held closely to His heart. The Lord understands our frailty as humans and expects nothing less. Put your faith in the only One who sees your value, be it in strength or weakness.

128

God Never Gets Weary

Don't you know? Haven't you been listening?
Yahweh is the one and only everlasting God,
the Creator of all you can see and imagine! He
never gets weary or worn out. His intelligence is
unlimited; he is never puzzled over what to do!
ISAIAH 40:28 TPT

It's important to understand that our God never gets weary. He doesn't get worn out by you or the craziness of your life. Even when you're full of drama and inconsolable, God isn't exhausted by it. You're not too much or too little. He knows you and loves you unfailingly.

Even more, God knows the complexity of your emotions, how to remedy the situation, and He will see it through to solution. He sees everything in its entirety and from every angle. So, your faith can be unshakable because God is unshakable. Let His absolute understanding and endurance secure your heart today.

129

Let God Be Your Song

The Eternal is my strength and my song,
and He has come to save me; He is my
God, and I will praise Him. He is the God
of my father, and I will exalt Him.
EXODUS 15:2 VOICE

Have you found yourself humming a song absentmindedly? Maybe you heard a catchy song and have been singing it ever since? Music matters to us, and it has a way of positively affecting our mood. We all have songs we hold close because they remind us of important moments. So what might it mean for God to be your song?

Could it mean He is always on your mind? Or might it signal God has imprinted on your heart? Maybe it means His Word is always on your lips, ready to spill forth at the right time? Regardless, celebrate God being your song, praising as He steadies your faith with constant reminders of His goodness.

130

A Heart of Gratitude

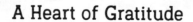

Seek the LORD and His strength; seek His face
continually [longing to be in His presence].
Remember [with gratitude] His marvelous
deeds which He has done, His miracles
and the judgments from His mouth.

1 CHRONICLES 16:11-12 AMP

It's one thing to remember God's goodness, but it's another to remember His marvelous works with heartfelt gratitude. Just like any loving parent, God desires to hear a grateful heart from His children. Saying *thank you* goes a long way. And when we take a moment to recognize kindness and generosity, it shows a maturity of faith in the believer.

Ask God to create in you an awareness of answered prayer. Ask for eyes to see the move of His hand in your circumstances. Learn to be watchful as you wait for answers. And watch how your intentionality grows an unshakable faith in your heart, knowing God is active in your life every day.

131

Making Peace with Our Weaknesses

He said to me, "My grace is enough for you, because power is made perfect in weakness." So I'll gladly spend my time bragging about my weaknesses so that Christ's power can rest on me. Therefore, I'm all right with weaknesses, insults, disasters, harassments, and stressful situations for the sake of Christ, because when I'm weak, then I'm strong.

2 Corinthians 12:9–10 ceb

Let's decide to make peace with our weaknesses. While that mindset goes against groupthink and what society says is acceptable, we're not to focus on pleasing the world. Our allegiance lies with God and is visible through our unshakable faith. We don't need to impress others; we need to obey the Lord. And if the Word says our weakness allows His power to be made perfect through us, then we embrace our humanity in humility.

You don't have to have it all figured out. What an unexpected blessing.

132

On the Battlefield Together

"Listen, Israel! Today you're going to fight a battle against your enemies. Don't be intimidated by them! Don't be afraid! Don't run away! Don't let them terrify you! The Eternal, your True God, has come out here with you, and He'll fight for you against your enemies and save you."

DEUTERONOMY 20:3-4 VOICE

Sometimes we have no option but to go into battle with others. It may be at a school board meeting or in a court of law or at our workplace, and there's just no way around it. We must stand up for what's right. We need to say what needs to be said. And it can intimidate us into inaction.

But once again, God reminds us of His powerful promise. We won't be alone as the fight ensues. Instead, He'll be on the battlefield fighting with us. Stand with confident faith because God will never leave your side.

133

Relying on God to Strengthen

He empowers the feeble and infuses the
powerless with increasing strength.
ISAIAH 40:29 TPT

Few things tangle our insecurities like feeling frail and delicate. When it seems we're incapable of handling hard circumstances, our self-esteem takes a beating. And because we have a million things on our plate, being ineffective is the worst. Every time these feelings come creeping in, let it be a red flag warning that we're working in our own strength.

What keeps you from leaning on the Lord when you feel feeble and powerless? As a believer, can you identify why you're choosing to not rely on God to strengthen you for the situation? When He created you, God had full understanding of your limitations, and His plan all along was to fill in the gap humanity left. So stand firm in your faith, embracing your Father's help, as you navigate those times of vulnerability.

134

Being Confident and Unafraid

"Behold—God is my salvation! I am
confident, unafraid, and I will trust in you."
Yes! The Lord Yah is my might and my
melody; he has become my salvation!
ISAIAH 12:2 TPT

Unshakable faith means you're confident in God and unafraid of the world. It means you trust His plan rather than panicking. You're certain He's working in your situation for your good and His glory. You're patient, knowing God never tarries. And you are full of hope because you believe He knows your needs and will meet them.

If this doesn't describe you right now, have faith that it can. Ask the Lord to make you a brave and confident believer. Trust that God is true to His word and won't ever leave you to figure things out alone. Ask for unshakable faith so you're able to stand strong as life comes at you.

135

Encouraging Steadfast Faith in Others

*In that glorious day, you will say to one another,
"Give thanks to the Lord and ask him for more!
Tell the world about all that he does! Let them
know how magnificent he is!" Sing praises to the
Lord, for he has done marvelous wonders, and
let his fame be known throughout the earth!*

ISAIAH 12:4-5 TPT

Consider that your steadfast faith is exactly what may encourage another's faith to become the same. When you speak confidently about God and His magnificence, it stirs the spirit of others. And every time you open up and share about the Lord's provision in your circumstances, hope springs forth in the heart of the needy. It's a privilege to speak of His fame to those around us!

Look for opportunities to sing God's praises. Be vocal in gratitude for His blessings. Encourage others to see His wonders in their own life!

136

Growing Strangely Dim

*Whom have I in heaven [but You]? And besides
You, I desire nothing on earth. My flesh and
my heart may fail, but God is the rock and
strength of my heart and my portion forever.*

Psalm 73:25–26 AMP

For many of us, the older we get, the less we desire earthly things. We see the decay of what we once held dear. We feel the pull on our heart to be with the Father in heaven. And what was once so important has faded over time. Looking through the lens of faith, age brings a longing unanswered by worldly offerings. And it reveals an anchored trust in God and our eternity with Him.

Let the things of this earth grow strangely dim as you focus your heart on heaven. Keep your eyes on God's promises, and let them be what anchors you to truth. Find comfort in knowing this is not your home.

137

Closer

But I'll keep coming closer and closer to you,
Lord Yahweh, for your name is good to me.
I'll keep telling the world of your awesome
works, my faithful and glorious God!

PSALM 73:28 TPT

The harder life gets, the closer we need to be to our God. He's the only One who can bring us comfort in difficult times. His peace can cover our anxious heart and bring rest when we need it the most. Although we sometimes hide away and try to figure things out on our own, we need God's presence more than anything else. It's how our faith becomes unshakable.

Thank God for being willing to wrap His Fatherly arms around you in reassurance and consolation. At the same time, let others know of His faithfulness so that in their time of need, they will remember the blessings that come from a steadfast faith in God.

138

Feet like a Deer

*Then I will still rejoice in the Eternal! I will rejoice
in the God who saves me! The Eternal Lord is
my strength! He has made my feet like the feet
of a deer; He allows me to walk on high places.*

HABAKKUK 3:18–19 VOICE

What does it mean to you personally to be able to walk
on high places? In your opinion, why would it be a good
thing for God to make your feet like that of a deer?

Think of the rugged terrain a deer traverses each day.
Imagine the valleys and mountaintops it travels. Consider
the hungry predators it must avoid and outwit. But the deer
has confidence in its God-given abilities. This animal is
self-assured and unwavering in its skills. Maybe the Lord
wants us to show the same confident faith, believing He
will give us all we need to navigate the ups and downs
life brings our way.

God's Lofty Commands

*Jesus said, "The first in importance is, 'Listen,
Israel: The Lord your God is one; so love the
Lord God with all your passion and prayer and
intelligence and energy.' And here is the second:
'Love others as well as you love yourself.' There is
no other commandment that ranks with these."*

MARK 12:29-31 MSG

Lofty, lofty, lofty! Even with unshakable faith and pure motives, we're unable to walk these commands out in acceptable ways. They demand a daily surrender to God as we ask Him to love through us. It's the best we can muster in our flesh.

Let God strengthen you to follow these commands. With His help, you can love God with passion and prayer. You can love Him with your mind and energy. And when you believe Him to be faithful, you can confidently love others. Let God strengthen you every day to be who He's asking you to be.

140

Let Nothing Erode

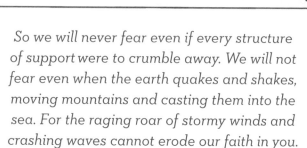

So we will never fear even if every structure of support were to crumble away. We will not fear even when the earth quakes and shakes, moving mountains and casting them into the sea. For the raging roar of stormy winds and crashing waves cannot erode our faith in you.

<small>PSALM 46:2-3 TPT</small>

Friend, let nothing dismantle your faith. No matter what hardships come your way, let your trust in God be unshakable. Difficulties should drive you into His arms, not from them. They should make you cling to God even more. Do they?

The psalmist makes a solid declaration of steadfastness, making known his strategy for life's storms. He recognizes they will come at you fast. He acknowledges the anxieties and worry they'll bring. But let today's scripture remind you that when fear threatens to crumble your foundation, shake your reality, or erode what you hold dear, your uncompromising faith will steady you.

141

The God Who Cannot Be Shaken

*God is in the midst of his city, secure and
never shaken. At daybreak his help will
be seen with the appearing of the dawn.*

PSALM 46:5 TPT

What a gift to know our God can never be shaken. Even with all the craziness of the world, He is unfazed. His sovereignty is irreplaceable and unmovable. Nothing surprises the Lord because He has full knowledge and complete control at all times. Even war, disease, famine, and natural disasters don't unsettle God's nerves, because He can see the whole picture.

Why is this so amazing? In those moments when we're struggling, we can trust God to be our strong anchor. He will steady our fearful heart. We can cling to Him for hope when we have none. Friend, knowing God cannot be shaken when our world feels chaotic provides a sense of comfort and peace—something unattainable any other way.

142

His Magnitude of Greatness

*Everyone look! Come and see the breathtaking
wonders of our God. For he brings both
ruin and revival. He's the one who makes
conflicts end throughout the earth, breaking
and burning every weapon of war.*

PSALM 46:8–9 TPT

It's hard to imagine anyone ending conflicts as big and important as the ones facing the world, especially when we struggle to calm the raging seas in our own lives. But once we begin to recognize the magnitude of greatness God possesses and how His wonders bless those who love Him, our faith will become unshakable. We'll find the strength to trust the Lord with our delicate circumstances.

Believe God will handle you with care. He knows why your heart is troubled and how to move forward in healing. Your Father loves with grace and precision, so you can trust Him to always have your best in mind. Let your faith be anchored to His greatness.

143

Why We Surrender

*Surrender your anxiety. Be still and realize
that I am God. I am God above all the nations,
and I am exalted throughout the whole
earth. Here he stands! The Commander!
The mighty Lord of Angel Armies is on our
side! The God of Jacob fights for us!*

PSALM 46:10-11 TPT

If you want to stand strong in the face of difficulties, surrender your anxieties to God. If you want to experience unexplained peace while in spine-weakening moments, give your burdens to the Lord. Every time you choose to let go of control, you're recognizing that God is God and you are not. Your decision to be still in the chaos will produce an unshakable faith in the One who can bring resolution.

Living this way takes intentionality and trust. It's a daily decision. It's a situational surrender. But God will give you the courage and confidence to walk it out if you ask.

A Divine Opportunity for Refreshment

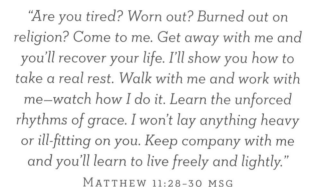

"Are you tired? Worn out? Burned out on religion? Come to me. Get away with me and you'll recover your life. I'll show you how to take a real rest. Walk with me and work with me—watch how I do it. Learn the unforced rhythms of grace. I won't lay anything heavy or ill-fitting on you. Keep company with me and you'll learn to live freely and lightly."

MATTHEW 11:28-30 MSG

Doesn't this offer sound delightful? Maybe right now this is exactly what you need to regroup. This is your longing and desire. Because you're battling exhaustion and frustration, a divine opportunity for refreshment feels unmatched.

But it takes steadfast faith to step out of life for a moment and into the arms of God. Why? Taking time away from a busy calendar is only doable when we know He will make good on His promises. We can trust the Way Maker.

145

No Longer Grieving the Past

Go back to your homes, and prepare a feast.
Bring out the best food and drink you have, and
welcome all to your table, especially those who
have nothing. This day is special. It is sacred to
our Lord. Do not grieve over your past mistakes.
Let the Eternal's own joy be your protection!
NEHEMIAH 8:10 VOICE

After reading the law of Moses to the Israelites, expos-
ing their blatant disobedience, Ezra instructed them to
observe the day as a celebratory moment rather than a
day of mourning. They had to choose to rejoice rather
than harp on all they had done wrong. This took a new
measure of faith.

It's easy to focus on our shortcomings. But as believers
who understand Jesus' death on the cross canceled every
sin, we must embrace that truth—that gift. And rather than
focus on our iniquities, choose joy and gratitude instead.

146

Unyielding and Impenetrable

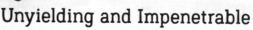

*The LORD will give [unyielding and
impenetrable] strength to His people; the
LORD will bless His people with peace.*
PSALM 29:11 AMP

Too often, we don't believe God will give us what we're asking for. We think ourselves too broken or sinful, so we try to figure things out on our own. But imagine the confidence you could muster if you believed God had blessings for you. He offers unyielding strength, meaning it can't give way to pressure. It can't be swayed. Add to that the kind of strength that's impenetrable, unable to be breached, and you're able to have unshakable faith.

With this, think of how differently you'd approach difficult circumstances. Consider the peace and joy you'd have because of it. Reflect on the changes you'd see in relationships as you navigate circumstances with steadfast faith in the Lord. When you ask God for strength rather than depend on yourself, it changes everything.

147

Nothing

*Jesus answered them, "Do you finally believe?
In fact, you're about to make a run for it—saving
your own skins and abandoning me. But I'm not
abandoned. The Father is with me. I've told you
all this so that trusting me, you will be unshakable
and assured, deeply at peace. In this godless
world you will continue to experience difficulties.
But take heart! I've conquered the world."*

JOHN 16:31-33 MSG

Unshakable faith brings deep peace. It allows you to face difficult times and not be pulled underwater. It brings an assuredness that reminds you that God's presence is always with you, be it in the dark valleys or on the mountaintops. And with the craziness of the world, it's a welcomed promise fulfilled by our belief in God's sovereignty.

There's nothing in this world stronger than God. No one smarter. No governments wiser. No plans or procedures cleverer. Anchor your faith in Him alone. God will steady you.

148

Steering Us

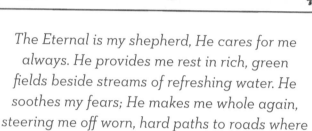

The Eternal is my shepherd, He cares for me always. He provides me rest in rich, green fields beside streams of refreshing water. He soothes my fears; He makes me whole again, steering me off worn, hard paths to roads where truth and righteousness echo His name.

PSALM 23:1–3 VOICE

Among the wonderful attributes of God, we can trust He is the great Course Corrector. When we follow Him, God will redirect us from the difficult paths we've walked for so long. His care and compassion will be with us always. And God will provide timely refreshment and rest to nourish our souls.

What is required of us? To invest in our relationship with the Lord so our faith grows and strengthens, becoming immovable as we navigate the ebbs and flows of life. The closer we are to God, the stronger our resolve to let Him be the leader of our life and steer us into righteousness.

149

Comforted in the Dark Moments

*Even in the unending shadows of death's
darkness, I am not overcome by fear. Because
You are with me in those dark moments, near with
Your protection and guidance, I am comforted.*
PSALM 23:4 VOICE

What a comfort to know God is with us in the dark moments. So often, we feel all alone in them. But to understand our heavenly Father is right there, protecting us as He guides us through, will bring unmatched comfort if we'll let it. And it takes faith not only to believe it but to wholeheartedly embrace it too.

As believers, we can't allow ourselves to give in to fear, because it reveals a lack of faith. Even when we're facing unending shadows and dark moments, we can find lasting peace through the Lord's presence. He will strengthen us when we ask! So choose today to have unshakable faith, knowing God is with you always.

150

Trusting God to Meet Your Needs

*You spread out a table before me, provisions
in the midst of attack from my enemies;
You care for all my needs, anointing my
head with soothing, fragrant oil, filling my
cup again and again with Your grace.*

PSALM 23:5 VOICE

It's hard to trust people to meet all our needs. Why? Because chances are it's never happened. We've never been fully cared for by someone. They may meet most of our emotional needs but fall short with financial support. Maybe they've been helpful to meet basic necessities but haven't encouraged us spiritually.

When God's Word says He will care for *all* your needs, that's exactly what He promises to do. Friend, you can anchor your faith in that powerful pledge every day. God will provide, filling your cup again and again with what you need to thrive. Look to Him alone, and watch how your anxious heart finds peace and hope.

151

Knowing God Pursues

*Certainly Your faithful protection and
loving provision will pursue me where I
go, always, everywhere. I will always be
with the Eternal, in Your house forever.*

PSALM 23:6 VOICE

As women, we long to be pursued. We want others to want
to know us because it's one of our deepest heart needs.
It makes us feel lovable and necessary. We feel important and valued. And honestly, it's rare to find someone
who loves us with such a passion. Rarely do we feel pursued by others, and it leaves a deep longing inside.

Knowing that God promises to be faithful in His love
and pursuit can steady us and bring a sense of peace.
Scripture says that no matter what, God will consistently
show His desire for us through protection and pursuit. Let
that be the strong foundation of your faith, reminding you
of your immeasurable value to the Father.

152

Rest and Trust

*The Eternal is the source of my strength and
the shield that guards me. When I learn to rest
and truly trust Him, He sends His help. This is
why my heart is singing! I open my mouth to
praise Him, and thankfulness rises as song.*

PSALM 28:7 VOICE

Did you catch that? God's help is available, but you have
a part to play. He will be the source of your strength and
the shield that guards, but you must take a leap of faith,
and it is learned behavior.

God wants us to rest and trust. It's a call for unshakable
faith because we're giving up control and believing in Him
for help instead. We can't rest if we're trying to save the
world. And we can't trust if we think our way is better
than His. Ask God for help so you can end each day with
praise and thanksgiving for all He has done!

153

Inner Strength

You will be the inner strength of all your people,
Yahweh, the mighty protector of all, and the
saving strength for all your anointed ones.
Save your people whom you love, and bless
your chosen ones. Be our shepherd leading us
forward, forever carrying us in your arms!

PSALM 28:8-9 TPT

God is responsible for your inner strength. He is the One who fills the gap left by our human limitations. When we feel weak and pray for God's help, He is the burst of intensity that boosts us forward. He's the surge of power we feel to take the next step. Yes, we are the ones blessed by His promises to protect and strengthen us for the battle.

Be quick to cry out to God when circumstances feel insurmountable. Hang your expectations on Him, trusting He'll infuse you for that meaningful moment. Your faith in His help can be steadfast. God will always come through for you.

Say It

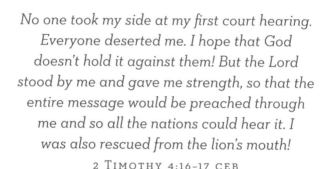

*No one took my side at my first court hearing.
Everyone deserted me. I hope that God
doesn't hold it against them! But the Lord
stood by me and gave me strength, so that the
entire message would be preached through
me and so all the nations could hear it. I
was also rescued from the lion's mouth!*

2 TIMOTHY 4:16-17 CEB

When you've got something to say, say it. When the Lord puts words in your mouth or a message on your heart to share, do so even if your knees are knocking. Even with sweaty hands, stand strong in your faith and speak. If God has called you to it, trust He'll give you the confidence to do it. Your job is to take that step of faith out of your comfort zone as you trust God.

Let Him be the One to strengthen you for the calling placed on your life. He's all you need.

155

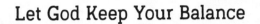

Let God Keep Your Balance

*I was pushed back, attacked so that I was
about to fall, but the Eternal was there to
help me keep my balance. He is my strength,
and He is the reason I sing; He has been
there to save me in every situation.*

PSALM 118:13-14 VOICE

Let God be what keeps you balanced. When you cling to Him, you'll be kept in perfect peace. He will help you navigate the ups and downs so you land in a place of stability. Regardless of the circumstances surrounding you, God is with you always. He'll catch you when you fall, because He is your strength.

Let the Lord turn your unsteady fear into unshakable faith. Watch in expectation as God brings you into perfect alignment with His love. And, friend, never doubt His ability to balance your heart to perfection. God will be a safety net when life gets messy.

156

Wide, Open Spaces

*When trouble surrounded me, I cried out to
the Eternal; He answered me and brought
me to a wide, open space. The Eternal is with
me, so I will not be afraid of anything. If God
is on my side, how can anyone hurt me?*

PSALM 118:5-6 VOICE

This passage of scripture paints a beautiful picture of being
rescued. So often when facing hard times, we feel squished
on all sides. It seems as if the walls are closing in. And we
sometimes end up in a panic, struggling to catch a deep
breath. So, learning God will answer our cries for help by
bringing us into a wide, open space is powerful imagery.

Hold tight to this amazing promise, and let it be what
securely anchors your faith to God. He always knows just
what you need and always at the right time. Instead of
giving in to the difficult circumstances, remember God
is on your side.

157

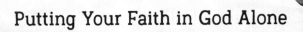

Putting Your Faith in God Alone

*It is better to put your faith in the Eternal
for your security than to trust in people.
It is better to put your faith in Him for
your security than to trust in princes.*
PSALM 118:8-9 VOICE

Chances are we're all guilty of putting our trust in people. It could be the president, our pastor, the CEO of a company, our parents, or our husband. There are certain people we decide are worthy of our allegiance, so we choose to follow their lead—hook, line, and sinker. In our minds, they are a savior of sorts. And as wonderful as they may be, they're no substitution for God.

He's the only One who will never let you down. He won't ever leave you. That means you can fearlessly anchor your faith in the Lord. He knows all, sees all, and will always be your safe place.

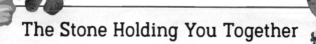

158

The Stone Holding You Together

*I will praise You because You answered me
when I was in trouble. You have become
my salvation. The stone that the builders
rejected has become the very stone that
holds together the entire foundation.*

PSALM 118:21-22 VOICE

What a powerful passage of scripture. Once we begin to understand the magnificence of God and the depth of His compassion, it's hard to imagine He was rejected for it. The Lord is the very cornerstone of our faith that makes us whole. It's from there that everything else in our life should be built.

Make sure God is at the very center of your life. Let Him be the One you place your trust in. Lavishly praise Him for His great faithfulness. Cry to God for His help. Starting today, let the Lord make your faith unshakable by recognizing He is the stone holding you together.

159

All You Need to Do

All I need to do is to call on you, Yahweh,
the praiseworthy God. When I do, I'm safe
and sound in you—delivered from my foes!

PSALM 18:3 TPT

It may be hard to believe the simplicity of today's verse. So often, we complicate faith by adding to it. We bring rules and regulations never sanctioned by God. And when we do, our faith gets rocked because we tie performance to it. But the Lord asks us to trust in Him above all else, and that belief opens the door to beautiful blessings.

Friend, your cry to God won't go unanswered. When life hits hard, let Him hear your heart. He will bring you into a safe place. And as you continue to ask for God's help, your faith will grow steadfast each time you see His hand move in your life.

160

The One Who Delights in You

Even though I was helpless in the hands of my hateful, strong enemy, you were good to deliver me. When I was at my weakest, my enemies attacked—but the Lord held on to me. His love broke open the way, and he brought me into a beautiful, broad place. He rescued me—because his delight is in me!

PSALM 18:17-19 TPT

Maybe you feel no one delights in you. Maybe you've lost important relationships because of betrayal. Maybe others have repeatedly abandoned or rejected you, and you're feeling unlovable. Broken. Unworthy.

God is the only One who can steady a heart and bring redemption. He promises to deliver you. He'll hold you securely in the storms. And when your faith rests in the Lord, His love will rewrite the messages that tell you you're worthless. God delights in you. He knows you fully and completely, and He delights in you!

161

An Unshakable God

Yahweh lives! Praise is lifted high to the unshakable God! Towering over all, my Savior-God is worthy to be praised! Look how he pays back harm to all who harm me, subduing all who come against me. He rescues me from my enemies; he lifts me up high and keeps me out of reach, far from the grasp of my violent foe.

PSALM 18:46–48 TPT

Be comforted knowing God is unshakable. He's immovable. The Lord is unwavering, committed to following through on every promise made. His love for you is steadfast. God's heart for you is faithful always. His plans for good are dependable and firm. And the Lord is trustworthy in all things.

Friend, this is why your faith in God can be unshakable. He is for you. The Lord is with you. And no matter what you're facing or feeling, God will deliver you without fail. So rise up in thanksgiving for His persistent compassion.

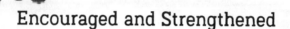

162

Encouraged and Strengthened

*David was greatly distressed, for the men spoke
of stoning him because the souls of them all
were bitterly grieved, each man for his sons
and daughters. But David encouraged and
strengthened himself in the Lord his God.*

1 SAMUEL 30:6 AMPC

Maybe you're in a state of distress right now. Maybe your
relationships are bogged down with bitterness, leaving
you feeling hopeless. Or maybe you've suffered great loss
and are angry and resentful about it. Life is anything but
fair. David had firsthand knowledge of that, but he knew
what to do about it.

David knew God was the answer—nothing else—so he
pressed into his Lord for encouragement and strength.
He went right to the Source to meet his pressing needs.
Let this be your story too! Let God see your unshakable
faith revealed through your choice to trust Him above all
else. Encourage and strengthen yourself in God alone.

163

God Is a Warrior

"The LORD your God is in your midst,
a Warrior who saves. He will rejoice over
you with joy; He will be quiet in His love
[making no mention of your past sins],
He will rejoice over you with shouts of joy."

We often think of God as meek and mild. We find comfort knowing He's gentle. We revel in His love, imagining our Father wrapping His arms around us. Although these thoughts are accurate and beautiful, let's not forget God is also a powerful Warrior! There's a magnificent strength and wildness about Him that can't be tamed. And He is mighty to save.

From His sweetness to His sovereignty, God is in your midst. He will both rescue and rejoice in His perfect timing. And as your faith becomes securely fastened in the Lord, you'll find an unshakable peace for your soul that's unmatched by anything the world can offer.

God's Peace Is Not Fragile

*"I leave the gift of peace with you—my peace.
Not the kind of fragile peace given by the world,
but my perfect peace. Don't yield to fear or be
troubled in your hearts—instead, be courageous!"*

JOHN 14:27 TPT

Have you ever considered that the peace offered by the world is. . .*fragile?* It's a flimsy substitute that doesn't hold up well under pressure. It is full of holes and heartaches. When life feels chaotic, we need sturdy peace rather than the kind that crumbles and shakes. So when scripture says God gives us His peace as a gift, it's a big deal. It's perfect in every way, and it allows us to be fearless rather than fearful.

Friend, you have full access to God's peace in your life. Regardless of what you're facing, He can be what settles your spirit and strengthens your soul. Let His faithfulness make your faith unshakable.

165

Time and Time Again

*At the very moment I called out to you, you
answered me! You strengthened me deep within
my soul and breathed fresh courage into me.*

PSALM 138:3 TPT

Life is challenging, and every day we're forced to face
heartbreaking situations and scary circumstances. There's
an epidemic of guilt and grief and gloom across the nation
and the world. And unless we embrace faith and let God
grow it into a steadfast force in our life, we'll crumble
under the weight of worry. We'll be weak and ineffective,
unable to live the way God intended.

But, friend, the Lord hears your cry for help! As your
voice calls God's name, He'll strengthen you for battle.
He will give power for His purposes. God will bring fresh
courage to your weary bones. And as you receive it time
and time again, your faith will become unshakable because
you will see His faithfulness.

166

Alive and Revived

By your mighty power I can walk through any devastation, and you will keep me alive, reviving me. Your power set me free from the hatred of my enemies. You keep every promise you've ever made to me! Since your love for me is constant and endless, I ask you, Lord, to finish every good thing that you've begun in me!

PSALM 138:7-8 TPT

What devastation have you walked through? A divorce or the loss of someone you loved? Maybe a diagnosis or a financial setback. We all face crushing moments, but clinging to God through them empowers us in beautiful ways.

Scripture says we can get through these times because the Lord will sustain us. He'll meet every need. God will revive us throughout the journey so we have strength and might to find resolution. Let this promise make your faith in Him unshakable. With God, you have everything you need.

167

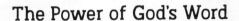

The Power of God's Word

*God means what he says. What he says goes.
His powerful Word is sharp as a surgeon's
scalpel, cutting through everything, whether
doubt or defense, laying us open to listen and
obey. Nothing and no one can resist God's Word.
We can't get away from it—no matter what.*

HEBREWS 4:12-13 MSG

God's Word is powerful and complete. There's nothing to add to it or remove from it. It can both convict and encourage, guiding every believer into a deeper relationship with the Lord. And in its pages, we can trust every word of what God says to be true and accurate. The Bible is unchanging. So you can confidently anchor your faith in His promises.

Do you read God's Word regularly? Is it a source of comfort and wisdom? If you'll let it, the Bible will be what steadies your heart and firms up your faith in the Lord.

168

Renewed Every Day

*So we aren't depressed. But even if our bodies
are breaking down on the outside, the person
that we are on the inside is being renewed
every day. Our temporary minor problems
are producing an eternal stockpile of glory
for us that is beyond all comparison.*
2 Corinthians 4:16–17 CEB

What a relief to know we can be renewed daily through our faith in God. We may have been wretched yesterday, mean-spirited, and rude. We may have been filled with debilitating fear that made us anxious. Maybe we were overwhelmed by life's decisions. But when we go to God with these heart issues, we find deep replenishment.

It doesn't matter what we're facing. He promises to renew us on the inside. God will give us new hope, fresh energy, extra grace, and more compassion when we ask. You can confidently anchor your faith in His promise to renew daily.

169

Where Is Your Focus?

*We don't focus on the things that can be
seen but on the things that can't be seen.
The things that can be seen don't last, but
the things that can't be seen are eternal.*

2 CORINTHIANS 4:18 CEB

This is a call for you to have a heavenly perspective rather than an earthly one. Too often, we focus on what our eyes can see. Marital issues. Global frustrations. Parenting challenges. Financial strains. Health worries. Grief and loss. Our places of lacking. Upcoming changes. And rather than trust God with them, we become obsessed and overwhelmed in our own strength.

But if your faith is unshakable—if you believe God *is* who He says and will *do* as He says—then your eyes will naturally focus on Him. Your heart will expect God's hand to move in your circumstances, and the difficulties of life won't overpower you.

Don't Tamper with God's Word

*Instead, we reject secrecy and shameful actions.
We don't use deception, and we don't tamper
with God's word. Instead, we commend ourselves
to everyone's conscience in the sight of God
by the public announcement of the truth.*

2 Corinthians 4:2 ceb

Let God's Word stand on its own. Never buy into the lie saying it's incomplete or lacking; it's God-breathed and finished. There are no books to add to it nor any scriptures that should be removed. His Word isn't contained in the Bible—His Word *is* the Bible. Don't tamper with it in any way.

Choose to be steadfast in your belief that God's Word is divinely inspired. Trust it to be whole and perfect. And let it be your source for answers, guidance, encouragement, and conviction so you can live righteously in the eyes of the Lord. Let His Word be your anchor to truth.

Contentment

*So be content with who you are, and don't
put on airs. God's strong hand is on you; he'll
promote you at the right time. Live carefree
before God; he is most careful with you.*

1 PETER 5:6–7 MSG

When our hope is secured in the Lord, we can be secure in our identity. And when we know who we are and whose we are, we can find contentment. Our unsettled heart can rest knowing we're loved and valued. And embracing that life-giving truth encourages a deeper relationship with God, creating a strong and steadfast faith.

You don't have to be someone different to be accepted. There's no need to put on airs to impress others. Let your worth be anchored in God alone. Live your life knowing you're completely loved and cherished by the One who created you. Let the Lord bring you closer, wrapping His arms around you. Choose to trust God's care and compassion.

172

The Truth Teller

Be well balanced and always alert, because your
enemy, the devil, roams around incessantly, like
a roaring lion looking for its prey to devour.

1 PETER 5:8 TPT

Many of us try to live in a land of unicorns, puppies, and rainbows. It's a wonderful place where everything is *good* because we bury our head in the sand and ignore anything unlovely. We refuse to acknowledge evil and choose to run from difficulties. But in the end, we find ourselves deep in disillusionment as reality comes barreling our direction.

God is genuine in His Word. Every verse shared is accurate and fact. He wants us to understand there's a real enemy who has plans to destroy. Let this secure your faith, recognizing God is a truth teller. He can be trusted fully and completely. Let His dependability secure your faith in Him. Let God's Word be the anchor that keeps you grounded.

Catalyst for Courage

*Take a decisive stand against him and resist
his every attack with strong, vigorous faith.
For you know that your believing brothers
and sisters around the world are experiencing
the same kinds of troubles you endure.*

1 PETER 5:9 TPT

What a powerful reminder we're not alone. As believers, we're all facing the same kinds of troubles in our relationships, finances, and health. We wrestle with our worth. We're up to our eyeballs in guilt and shame. All around the world, those who follow the Lord are grappling with grief, loss, and other discouragement. Friend, you're not the only one struggling. Knowing you're in good company should bring a sense of solidarity.

Let that be a catalyst for courage. Your faith in God knits you and other believers together in meaningful ways. Harness that intimacy, and let it fuel your fight to stand strong in your belief, certain others are doing the same thing.

174

The Brief Season

*And then, after your brief suffering, the
God of all loving grace, who has called you
to share in his eternal glory in Christ, will
personally and powerfully restore you and
make you stronger than ever. Yes, he will
set you firmly in place and build you up.*

1 Peter 5:10 TPT

What does *brief* suffering mean to you? Most would probably hope for a twenty-four-hour period of time. We may agree to a week or month. But it's not up to us. God knows the exact amount of time necessary to complete His work in us, and it won't take a moment longer.

Romans 8:28 says, "God works all things together for good for the ones who love God." When we stand strong on that promise by faith, we trust He'll personally and powerfully restore us at the end of the *brief* season. We'll know without a doubt God will make us stronger.

175

The Power of Prayer

*Confess and acknowledge how you have
offended one another and then pray for one
another to be instantly healed, for tremendous
power is released through the passionate,
heartfelt prayer of a godly believer!*

JAMES 5:16 TPT

Have you ever considered that your prayers release power? Scripture says when a believer talks to God with honest and fervent prayers, it starts a chain reaction. That act of faith ignites a response of great power. It's His strength working through you, and it's a force of goodness that heals and restores in His name.

Believers with unshakable faith know their prayers have the weight necessary to steady their heart in every situation. They understand prayer is capable of healing every broken relationship. They recognize the muscle it provides every challenging circumstance. And it's that commitment to prayer that gives believers a steadfast faith because they know the power it releases.

176

Nothing Too Difficult or Too Wonderful

"Ah Lord God! Behold, You have made the heavens and the earth by Your great power and by Your outstretched arm! There is nothing too difficult or too wonderful for You."
Jeremiah 32:17 AMP

Since it was God who made the heavens and the earth and everything in them, don't you think He can manage your difficult circumstances? With words, God formed our existence. He spoke to nothingness and brought forth awesomeness. The Lord is fully capable of guiding you through any and every battle that comes your way.

Consider His magnificent power and strength. Think on God's sovereignty and dominion. Meditate on His love and compassion for you. Let these things be what firms up your faith in Him, making it unshakable. Just as scripture says, "There is nothing too difficult or too wonderful for [God]." Anchor your hope in that!

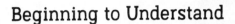

Beginning to Understand

Riches and glory come from you, you're ruler over all; you hold strength and power in the palm of your hand to build up and strengthen all. And here we are, O God, our God, giving thanks to you, praising your splendid Name.

1 CHRONICLES 29:12–13 MSG

When you truly begin to understand the awesomeness of God and all He can do in your life, the only response you'll have is praise. You'll be humbled by His splendor and majesty. To recognize all riches, glory, strength, and power come directly from God overwhelms our heart with an attitude of reverence. The Lord is good!

Friend, you don't have to work at having unshakable faith; you just need to spend time with God. Being in His presence daily opens your eyes to a deeper revelation of His grandeur. You'll gain a divine perspective of His promises for your life, and you will feel secured by God's love.

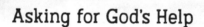

178

Asking for God's Help

*O Eternal One, show me how to live according to
Your statutes, and I will keep them always. Grant
me understanding so that I can keep Your law
and keep it wholeheartedly. Guide me to walk in
the way You commanded because I take joy in it.*

PSALM 119:33-35 VOICE

The psalmist's request is clear: He is asking God to
show him how to live. He wants a greater understanding
and guidance. Because the writer finds joy in following
God's commands—and because he recognizes that without
God's help, it's unattainable—he is imploring the Lord
for His assistance.

This is so important to understand. It's not up to us
to live righteously in our own strength. We don't have to
walk out our faith alone. We're simply not able to. But
when we anchor our trust to God and ask for His support
every day, an unshakable faith will emerge.

179

Underused Faith

*Because you have so little faith. I tell you
this: if you had even a faint spark of faith,
even faith as tiny as a mustard seed, you
could say to this mountain, "Move from here
to there," and because of your faith, the
mountain would move. If you had just a sliver
of faith, you would find nothing impossible.*

MATTHEW 17:20 VOICE

Today's verse offers a strong rebuke, but it's one laced with hope. We're being challenged to inspect the depth of our faith, because for many it's underused. We may believe things are possible when we trust God, but our faith often wavers.

When we're barely clinging to hope, God wants our belief to increase. He wants us to trust Him as Protector, Healer, Restorer, and Savior. God is requiring a steadfast faith because His power flows from it, and it will strengthen us to dig in and stand strong.

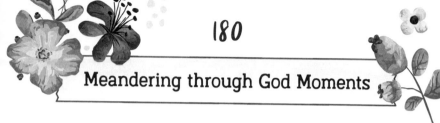

180

Meandering through God Moments

*But as for me, your strength shall be my song
of joy. At each and every sunrise, my lyrics of
your love will fill the air! For you have been my
glory-fortress, a stronghold in my day of distress.*

PSALM 59:16 TPT

Start each day praising God for His unmatched goodness displayed throughout your years. As you spend time unpacking the ways He's been dependable and trustworthy in your life, your own faith will find firm footing. Sometimes we need to be reminded of how God's hand has moved in challenging circumstances. We need to recall His steadfastness in our situations.

Every time you meander through God's moments of magnificence, it supernaturally strengthens your faith that He will do it again. Today, thank Him for being your song of joy. Show appreciation that He's been your glory-fortress and stronghold. And let it bolster your belief, making your faith unshakable.

Scripture Index

Exodus
15:2. 129

Deuteronomy
7:9. 56
20:3-4 132
32:4 69

Joshua
1:5, 7. 67
1:9. 68

1 Samuel
30:6 162

1 Chronicles
16:11-12. 130
28:20 109
29:12-13 177

Nehemiah
8:10 145

Psalms
16:1-2 119

16:5-6. 120
16:7-8 118
18:3. 159
18:17-19 160
18:46-48 161
23:1-3. 148
23:4 149
23:5 150
23:6 151
27:1. 123
27:2-3. 124
27:5-6 107
27:9 106
27:14. 105
28:7 152
28:8-9 153
29:11. 146
31:3-4. 110
46:2-3 140
46:5 141
46:8-9 142
46:10-11 143
59:16 180
73:25-26 136

73:28 137	Jeremiah
86:1–3. 63	29:11. 61
86:8–10 64	29:8–9 62
86:11. 65	29:12–13 60
86:12–13 66	32:17. 176
112:7 116	
118:5–6. 156	Lamentations
118:8–9. 157	3:22–24 39
118:13–14 155	
118:21–22 158	Habakkuk
119:33–35. 178	3:18–19 138
138:3 165	
138:7–8. 166	Zephaniah
	3:17. 163
Proverbs	
3:5–7. 41	
3:9–10 42	Matthew
3:11–12 43	6:31–32. 54
3:26–27 27	10:16. 121
28:1. 108	10:19–20 122
	11:28–30. 144
Isaiah	17:20. 179
12:2. 134	21:21 1
12:4–5. 135	21:22. 2
40:7–8 126	25:19–21 55
40:11. 127	
40:28. 128	Mark
40:29 133	5:36 112
40:31 125	11:22 14
41:10. 117	

11:23 10

11:24 12

12:29–31 139

Luke

16:10 35

John

5:8–9 102

12:42–43 101

14:27 164

15:7–8 100

16:31–33 147

Romans

8:26 98

8:28 99

8:31 96

8:35 97

10:9 6

10:10 8

10:17 4

12:2 90

12:3 91

12:9–10 92

12:12 95

12:14–16 93

12:17–19 94

1 Corinthians

1:9 44

1:28–29 46

6:19–20 89

10:13 37

13:4–7 53

16:13–14 104

2 Corinthians

1:4 84

1:6 85

1:11 86

1:21 87

1:22 88

4:2 170

4:16–17 168

4:18 169

5:6–7 22

5:14 24

12:9–10 131

Ephesians

2:4–5 18

2:8–9 16

2:10 20

6:10 113

6:14 114

6:18 115

Philippians

1:12 49
1:14 50
1:20 51
1:28–29. 52
4:13. 111

Colossians

1:22–23. 33

1 Thessalonians

4:1. 83
5:23–24 82

2 Thessalonians

3:2–3 81

2 Timothy

1:7 103
4:16–17 154

Hebrews

4:12–13. 167
10:22–23 45
10:24–25 47
10:38–39 48
11:1 5
11:3 7
11:6 3

11:7 11
11:8 13
11:11. 15
11:13 17
11:23 19
11:29 21
11:30. 23
12:1 58
12:12–13 59
12:28. 57
13:5. 79
13:6–7. 80
13:8. 77

James

1:2–4. 26
1:6. 28
1:12 30
1:13–14 32
1:17 34
1:21 36
1:22. 38
1:27 40
2:14. 25
4:7–8. 76
4:9–10 78
5:16. 175

1 Peter

5:6-7 171
5:8 172
5:9 173
5:10 174

2 Peter

1:3. 29
1:5-7 31

1 John

2:15-16 9
3:1. 73
3:16. 71
3:18-20 72
3:21. 74
3:23-24 75

3 John

5 70

Dig into God's Word!

180 Bible Verses for Conquering Anxiety

This compact book pairs 180 Bible verses each with a devotional thought that is equal parts practical and encouraging. Here you'll find the strength to conquer your fears, as your heart is anchored to a solid foundation of faith.

Paperback / 978-1-64352-961-5

180 Bible Verses for a Less Stressed Life

This compact book pairs 180 Bible verses each with a devotional thought that is equal parts practical and encouraging. Here you'll find more peace and less stress, as your heart is anchored to a solid foundation of faith.

Paperback / 978-1-63609-246-1